Rosa Luxemburg and the
Struggle for Democratic Renewal

T0386145

Rosa Luxemburg and the Struggle for Democratic Renewal

Jon Nixon

PLUTO PRESS

First published 2018 by Pluto Press
345 Archway Road, London N6 5AA

www.plutobooks.com

Copyright © Jon Nixon 2018

The right of Jon Nixon to be identified as the author of this work has
been asserted by him in accordance with the Copyright, Designs and
Patents Act 1988.

British Library Cataloguing in Publication Data
A catalogue record for this book is available from the British Library

ISBN   978 0 7453 3652 7   Hardback
ISBN   978 0 7453 3647 3   Paperback
ISBN   978 1 7868 0194 4   PDF eBook
ISBN   978 1 7868 0228 6   Kindle eBook
ISBN   978 1 7868 0227 9   EPUB eBook

Typeset by Stanford DTP Services, Northampton, England
Printed and bound by CPI Group (UK) Ltd, Croydon, CR0 4YY
Simultaneously printed in the United Kingdom and United States of America

for
Pauline

Contents

Preface

There are many Rosa Luxemburgs: the legendary 'Red Rosa' of the barricades; the tragic victim of historical forces beyond her control; the closet anarchist who celebrated 'spontaneity' at the expense of organised action; the unwitting stooge of the Bolsheviks; the martyr to state violence and political opportunism; the apostate who dared to question the precepts of orthodox Marxism ... But there is also the Rosa Luxemburg, who thought her way through one of the most critical periods of German history and for whom thinking formed the basis of political action. This is the Rosa Luxemburg with whom this book is concerned.

The problem that Luxemburg grappled with throughout her life was how to reconcile her deep commitment to two traditions of political thought and action: democracy and socialism. Was it possible to be a democrat when democracy had become a cover for protecting and reproducing the privilege of the ruling elite? Was it possible to be a socialist when socialism relegated the proletariat to the status of foot soldiers under the leadership of a supposedly enlightened vanguard?

She inveighed against 'bourgeois democracy' and warned against the centralising tendencies inherent in socialism, but she never wavered in her belief that democratic socialism was a possibility. To think as a socialist, she maintained, is to view history from the perspective of the oppressed; to think as a democrat is to acknowledge the agency of the oppressed in the making of history; to think as a democratic socialist is to think – and act – in solidarity with the oppressed in the overcoming of their oppression.

To think in such a way is to think internationally and inter-culturally and to value the unpredictability and spontaneity of human agency. These twin themes – international solidarity and the spontaneity of revolutionary action – are the hallmarks of Luxemburg's thinking. They are her enduring legacy, but they only make sense in the light of her deeply humanistic strain of thought. If Luxemburg was a socialist and a democrat, she was also an uncompromising humanist in her insistence on the human potential for social and political transformation.

It was a transformation, she maintained, that could only be achieved through the consciousness of the oppressed: the economically impoverished, the politically disenfranchised and the socially excluded. It was only from the consciousness of the powerless that a more rational, humane and just society could emerge. They alone had the capacity to think the unthinkable.

What are we to make of this socialist, who took issue with the leading socialists of her time? This democrat, who inveighed against the moral and political bankruptcy of parliamentary democracy? This humanist, who rejected the individualistic assumptions implicit in the Enlightenment project? She was difficult – intriguingly difficult – but was she anything more than this? Did the difficulty that she presented in her own person and her own thinking add up to a critique from which we can learn and a sense of purpose from which we can move forward?

Our starting point is the work embedded in the life and the life embedded in the history: a complex and riven history that tore Europe apart, unleashed the unprecedented horrors of the First World War, and saw the re-emergence of fascism in the form of Nazism as a potential world power. Luxemburg stood at the tipping point of history as it dipped into the horrors of what Eric Hobsbawm termed 'the short twentieth century': the rough ground between the commencement of the First World War and the collapse of Communism. Luxemburg exited – not of her own free will – towards the beginning of that history but her life and work continue to resonate.

Chapters 1 and 2 provide an introduction to her life and work. Both these chapters are biographical in mode, while setting her life and work within a broad social, historical and political frame of reference. The central chapters of the book (Chapters 3–5) focus on and elaborate some of the major themes within her work: the nature of political struggle; the scope of political agency; and the dynamics of political purpose. Chapters 6 and 7 reflect on the traces she has left; the questions she continues to pose; and the ways forward to which she tentatively directs us.

Jon Nixon
Kendal, Cumbria
September 2017

Acknowledgements

I would like to thank David Castle and the team at Pluto Press for believing in this book and in my capacity to produce it. Thanks, also, to the anonymous reviewers whose comments were helpful, informative and insightful.

I owe a great debt of gratitude to Stewart Ranson whose friendship, encouragement and generosity have supported me throughout the drafting of this book. Fred Inglis's encouragement and support in the early stages of the project were also invaluable.

Thanks to Amy Robinson, Anne Corbett, Ari-Elmeri Hyvönen, Camilla Erskine, Claus Emmeche, Derek Heather, Di Ponti, Feng Su, Helen Gunter, Jae Park, Judith Ashman, Maha Bali, Margaret Wood, Marnie Holborow, Paul Gibbs, Ronald Barnett, Stephen Powell, Tamara Savelyeva, Tanya Fitzgerald, Wayne Veck and William Fisher for the good talk, intellectual friendship and support along the way. Without our ongoing – but necessarily intermittent – conversations, this book would have been 'thinner' in every way.

Dave Cope generously allowed me access to his superb archive of labour history and literature, while Derek Robinson kindly rooted out relevant books from his magnificent collection. Cumbria Library Service has – as always – proved an invaluable resource.

I remember, also, in gratitude, the late Dora Bannister, Harold Rosen, Jean Rudduck and Lawrence Stenhouse, who taught me some hard lessons in how to think and write.

Finally, my thanks to Pauline Nixon for being there, and, in her immense generosity of spirit, for allowing the space and time necessary for this project to come to fruition.

A Note to the Reader

I have, in the main, introduced individuals using their full name and thereafter referred to them by their surname – the exception being when a forename is required to distinguish individuals with the same surname or on the rare occasions when either a full name or forename seems appropriate within the given context. The Glossary is intended to help readers with historical references, frequently used acronyms relating to organisations and key individuals referred to more than once.

PART I

Taking History as it Comes

And finally, one must take history as it comes, whatever course it takes
Rosa Luxemburg, 11 January 1919, letter to Clara Zetkin (R: 492)

1

The Long Apprenticeship

She was born on 5 March 1871, in the small town of Zamość in the province of Lublin, part of Russian-occupied Poland near to the border of Ukraine. It had for centuries been on the vital trade route from northern Europe to the Black Sea. The large Jewish population was subject to special laws, excluded from most professions and in the main ghettoised. As her contemporary and collaborator, Paul Frölich put it: 'It was an out-of-the-way, backward world, a world of resignation and want' (2010[1939]: 1). Luxemburg's family – although Jewish – was set apart from this world by its comparative financial security and its educational aspirations. Her paternal grandfather had achieved a certain level of prosperity and financial independence through his involvement in the timber trade, which had taken him to Germany where her father had been educated and had become acquainted with liberal ideas and Western European literature. Her mother was also well read in both Polish and German literature. So, Luxemburg, the youngest of five children, was brought up within a family that – notwithstanding the general poverty of the local Jewish community – was comparatively stable, secure and secular.

In 1873, the family moved to Warsaw. She had a pronounced limp and in 1876 was wrongly diagnosed as suffering from tuberculosis. The wrong diagnosis led to the wrong treatment. As a consequence, she was confined for a year in a heavy plaster cast, which had no remedial effect whatsoever on her shrunken and misshaped leg. Indeed, her year-long confinement may well have prevented her body from adjusting to what seems in retrospect to have been a case of congenital hip dysplasia. Nevertheless, her early childhood seems to have been relatively happy. She rarely referred to these early years in later life but one might assume that, as the youngest in what seems to have been a caring and close-knit family, she was the focus of much attention from her older siblings and her parents. Her year-long confinement within the culturally and linguistically rich environment of her family may also have helped ensure that by the time she entered her teens she could read, speak and write in Russian, Polish, Hebrew and German.

The most highly regarded school in Warsaw was reserved for Russian children. So in 1884, Luxemburg applied for and won a scholarship to the Second Gymnasium – a single sex high school – where a limited number of places were allocated to Jews. All lessons and conversations within the school were conducted in Russian and the use of the Polish language – which for most pupils was their mother tongue – was strictly forbidden. After three years, she graduated with As in 14 subjects and Bs in five. This was an outstanding achievement that distinguished her academically from her fellow pupils. However, the gold medal that she would normally have been awarded as a mark of her distinction was withheld on the grounds that she had shown a rebellious attitude. To be labelled rebellious was – for a 16-year-old Jewish, Polish girl living in a deeply anti-Semitic, authoritarian and patriarchal society within Russian-occupied Poland – a serious matter. Luxemburg was already defining herself – and being defined – as an outsider.

Poland was in political turmoil. During the 1880s, the dominant revolutionary party was the *Narodnaya Volya* ('*People's Will*'), which had developed as a terrorist organisation from an earlier populist grouping. *Narodnaya Volya* was inspired by a utopian vision of Polish national regeneration through the peasantry. Following the assassination of Tsar Alexander II in 1881, a new party was founded – *Proletariat* ('Polish People') – with a view to creating a broad base of support, instead of relying exclusively on acts of individual terrorism. *Proletariat* was Poland's first socialist party and – following its foundation by Ludwik Waryński in 1881 – organised strikes in Warsaw and Łódź and a general strike in Żyradów in 1883. Large-scale arrests followed and in 1884 – the year Luxemburg entered high school – leading members of *Proletariat* were imprisoned. Four of the leaders were subsequently hanged in Warsaw, and Waryński was sentenced to 16 years' hard labour. Having survived three years of his sentence, he died in custody as Luxemburg was graduating from high school.

The savage sentences meted out to the leaders of *Proletariat* destroyed the party's existing support base and caused it to disband. A number of small groups continued to function: among them the Union of Polish Workers, the Association of Workers and the Second *Proletariat*. Although these were in the main disparate groupings, they shared with the now defunct *Proletariat* a determination to break with the terrorist tactics associated with the earlier *Narodnaya Volya*. By the time Luxemburg left school, she was in all likelihood already affiliated to socialist groups that were to form the nucleus of the Second *Proletariat*. To be associated with such groups – all of which operated beneath the radar screen of state surveillance – was a very risky business. From the perspective of her high school teachers, Luxemburg was – to draw on a contemporary analogy – at risk of 'radicalisation'.

For the next two years, she gained her political education – informally and covertly – through groups associated with the Second *Proletariat*. We know little about this phase of her life. But presumably, she was involved in both theoretical and tactical discussions around key issues of the day: for example, the relation between nationalism and socialism and the appropriate means of organising resistance within occupied territory. These discussions are likely to have been well informed and intellectually challenging. Luxemburg would have been in the company of socialists, who were well versed across a range of Marxist and socialist literatures and well practised in the organisational tactics of resistance. Although we know little of how she related to her family during this period – or of how they related to her – there is no evidence of any serious rupture. It is likely, therefore, that she continued to draw on the cultural richness of her own family background and perhaps, in particular, her mother's love of German literature.

She was coming under increasing state surveillance. This was undoubtedly a major push factor in her move to Zurich in 1889. She was clearly in danger. But there were also significant pull factors – not least the attraction of the University of Zurich as one of the few universities that admitted women. In addition, Zurich had a vibrant émigré community of political exiles and intellectual dissidents to which she would have been drawn. To head off alone and at the age of 19 for a new life in a new country must – even for someone who was fluent in three languages – have required immense *chutzpah*. There are tall tales of her crossing the border in a hay cart as a means of escape from political persecution. For all their romantic appeal, these apocryphal stories miss the point. She needed to get to Zurich to go on learning, to extend her intellectual reach, to achieve her academic potential and to be part of what for her was the vibrant centre of socialist debate. It is to the credit of her family that – as far as we know – they placed no obstacles in the way of what for her was both a welcome escape and an amazing opportunity.

Her move to Zurich coincided with the formation of the Second International (1889–1916): a key moment in the development of international socialism. The Second International provided an organisational framework – and a platform – for Luxemburg to sharpen her thinking, hone her rhetorical skills and assume a public presence on the radical left. Its collapse in 1916, following the outbreak of the First World War, was for Luxemburg and many of her comrades a personal tragedy as well as a political catastrophe. But in 1889, the world was all before her. Hers was no romantic vision whereby the collapse of capitalism would inevitably lead to the emergence of socialism. On the contrary, capitalism's inevitable collapse – as she saw it – would lead to barbarism unless the conditions necessary for socialism had been put in place. The Second International provided a forum within which socialists were able to debate what constituted those conditions and how they might be established.

At the University of Zurich, she enrolled initially in the faculty of philosophy and pursued courses in the natural sciences and mathematics. Within the field of natural sciences, she specialised in biology and zoology. Later she switched to the faculty of law – which included the social sciences – but her interest in the natural sciences remained with her throughout her life. Her facility – and delight – in mathematics combined with her studies in the social sciences led her into the field of economics and provided the focus for her doctoral research into industrial development within Poland. Twenty years later, she would build on the insights gained from this earlier analysis and make a major contribution to economic theory through her work on capital accumulation.

She also fell in love – deeply and complicatedly in love – with someone as emotionally complex and intellectually uncompromising as herself. Leo Jogiches was born in Vilnius, the capital of Lithuania, then part of the Russian Empire. He was four years older than Luxemburg. He was a superb tactician and had at his disposal the financial resources to fund the projects that would steer the Second International in what he believed to be the right direction. Throughout his life, he operated below the radar screen. He was undoubtedly a bit of a loner and no doubt politically and personally quite a controlling person. He possibly recognised in her the theoretician he might never be; she recognised in him the superb tactician of the Left from whom she needed to learn. Both probably perceived in the other something of what each possessed in abundance: the capacity for immense mental and physical courage.

In 1893, Luxemburg addressed the third congress of the Second International Congress in Zurich. She used the opportunity to distance herself from the Polish Socialist Party (PPS), which had been founded the previous year. Opposing the PPS, she argued against Polish independence and for collaboration between the Polish and Russian working class. In the same year, Jogiches established the journal *Sprawa Robotnicza* ('*The Workers' Cause*'), which was published in Paris. For the next five years, Luxemburg contributed regularly to the journal and made frequent visits to Paris to oversee its publication. She also used these visits to pursue her studies in the Polish libraries located in Paris. In 1894, Jogiches and Luxemburg – together with Julian Marchlewski and Adolph Warszawski – founded the Social Democracy and the Kingdom of Poland (SDKP) party as a breakaway from PPS. *Sprawa Robotnicza* became the main policy organ of SDKP, with Luxemburg (using the pseudonym R. Krusznyska) as its overall editor and one of its main contributors.

The final issue – Issue 24 – of *Sprawa Robotnicza* appeared in 1896. In its brief three-year publication span, it had mounted a sustained campaign against Polish nationalism and in support of international socialism. It had also helped to establish the SDKP as a political force within the Second International and to launch Luxemburg as a figure to be reckoned with in any debate on Polish nationalism and on the broader issue of the relation between nationalism and socialism. As a consequence, Luxemburg led the SDKP delegation at the Fourth Congress of the Second International in London. There she came under fierce personal attack, but the SDKP's existence as a separate member of the Second International was established and with it her own reputation as a serious political activist and tactician.

The following year she submitted her doctoral thesis, *The Industrial Development of Poland*, for examination (See CW I: 1–78). This was approved and Luxemburg became one of the first women in Europe to obtain a PhD in economics. Her thesis provided a detailed analysis of the development of capitalism in Poland and highlighted the impact of the global economy on industrialisation. She concluded,

> It is an inherent law of the capitalist method of production that it strives to materially bind together the most distant places, little by little, to make them economically dependent on each other, and eventually transform the entire world into one firmly joined productive mechanism.
>
> (CW I: 73)

Having already established herself as a serious activist, she was now beginning to gain recognition as a significant theorist within the context of the Second International – an intellectually challenging and politically charged context in which, as Tony Judt put it, 'you could not be important unless you were of theoretical standing' (Judt with Snyder 2012: 90).

Luxemburg's central insight into the global workings of the capitalist economy had implications that she would seek to elaborate for the rest of her life. Eventually it would enable her to theorise capitalism as inherently rapacious and exploitative, and to develop tactics of resistance based on the international solidarity of the working class and its capacity for collective action. By 1897, she had laid the foundations for these later achievements: she had gained academic recognition; she had learned how to edit, communicate in several languages, and manage complex printing schedules; how to speak publically; how to persuade and how to face down hostile criticism. She had also fallen in love with a man whom she respected but to whom she was financially and to some extent emotionally dependent and whose emotional detachment was a source of both fascination and frustration.

Zurich had served her well, but it was time to move on.

STRUGGLES *WITHIN* SOCIALISM

Berlin – the world's most industrialised city and the centre of European socialist politics – was the obvious destination. But there were practical problems to be overcome, not least of which was obtaining a residential permit. She speedily resolved this problem with the assistance of her friend Olympia Lübeck, whose son, Gustav, was persuaded by his mother to marry Luxemburg. The marriage, which was entirely one of convenience with the couple parting company on the doorstep of the registry office immediately after the ceremony, automatically granted her German citizenship. The other pressing problem was finding somewhere to live. This problem was exacerbated by her financial situation. Luxemburg had neither independent means nor a steady income and had relied heavily on Jogiches for financial support during her time in Zurich. In moving to Berlin, she would have to continue to rely on that support, at least for the foreseeable future. This placed her in the awkward position of relying financially on Jogiches and at the same time determining on a course of action that would require them to be physically apart from one another for significant stretches of time.

She remained deeply attached to Jogiches. A letter dated 17 May 1898 and written shortly after her arrival in Berlin expressed a torrent of conflicting emotions. The problem of finding somewhere permanent to live was clearly at the forefront of her concerns: 'The rooms are generally dreadfully expensive everywhere' (L: 39). Attempting to justify her expenditure, she goes into details regarding the relative costs of different rented accommodation in different parts of the city. She then shifts to her own sense of isolation: 'I feel as though I have arrived here as a complete stranger and all alone, to "conquer Berlin", and having laid eyes on it, I now feel anxious in the face of its cold power, completely indifferent to me' (L: 40).

She describes how she had been reflecting on their time together in Switzerland: 'when I turned my thoughts back for a moment to what I had left behind, what I saw was – an empty space ... We neither lived together nor did we find joy in one another' (L: 41). She writes of his 'stony heart' that is 'as constant and reliable as a cliff, but also just as hard and inaccessible'. Yet, in spite of these recriminations, she asks: 'Do you have any conception of how much I love you?' (L: 43).

Perhaps it was because Luxemburg was capable of such emotional intensity – and had the emotional honesty to acknowledge and express that intensity – that she was so resilient. Throughout her life, she displayed a remarkable combination of emotional receptivity and intellectual hard headedness. This possibly explains how, as a new arrival in Berlin and not withstanding her sense of isolation and emotional turmoil, she was able to establish herself with such assurance within the newly legalised Social Democratic Party of Germany (SPD), which having been banned under the Anti-Socialist Laws in 1878 regained legal status in 1890. Almost a quarter of the electorate – close to 1.8 million men – had voted SPD in the previous Reichstag elections that had been held in 1893. The most influential socialist movement in Europe with over 100,000 members, the SPD was on the threshold of a break-through in the forthcoming elections that were to be held later that year. Moreover, with over 90 socialist daily newspapers in circulation, there were ample opportunities for Luxemburg to further her career as a campaigning journalist and pamphleteer and thereby gain some measure of financial independence.

On arrival in Germany, she volunteered to campaign in the largely Polish-speaking area of Upper Silesia. This was no easy task. Upper Silesia was dominated by conservative Catholic mine workers and the SPD had no significant presence in the area. Luxemburg took on the task with characteristic vigour and determination. She seems still to have needed Jogiches' recognition, telling him in one of her frequent letters that: 'I am ... making my appearance as an outstanding public speaker' (L: 60). But she was clearly growing in confidence and independence and gaining not only the support of the electorate but also the respect of senior figures within the party. One of the reasons for her success was no doubt her positive and open response to Upper

Silesia: its geography, which she loved, its people with whom she could relate and its language, which was after all her own mother tongue. Later in that same letter to Jogiches, she tells him:

> You have no idea how happy it all makes me. I feel as though I've been born anew, as though I have the ground under my feet again. I can't get enough of listening to them speak, and I can't breathe in enough of the air here!
>
> (L: 62)

The elections were held in June 1898. Twenty-seven per cent of the electorate voted SPD, but this translated into only 14 per cent of the seats in the Reichstag. Clearly there was something deeply undemocratic at work in the parliamentary system – something reflected in the suffrage system and reinforced by the overriding power of extra-parliamentary elements such as the king, Kaiser Wilhelm, who held absolute power. The Reichstag ratified budgets, but otherwise had little power. The problem lay in the democratic deficit at the heart of the parliamentary system, and the solution – as Luxemburg saw it – could only lie in a socialist critique of that system and the demand for democratic socialism. The 1898 election defined the fault line between what Luxemburg called 'bourgeois democracy', namely, a non-democracy that protects the privilege of those with accumulated wealth and a democratic socialism that would challenge that protection of privilege and redistribute the accumulated wealth of the privileged minority. The presenting issue, for Luxemburg, was the manifest failure of the Reichstag as a genuinely democratic forum.

During the next ten years, as the SPD sought to reconcile its socialist ideals with its electoral success, deep divisions opened up – divisions that had been implicit in the party since its inception. Formed from the amalgamation of two rival parties, the SPD agreed at its inaugural conference in 1875, on a programme (the Gotha Programme) that largely reproduced the demands of the non-Marxist wing of the newly formed party. During the 1880s, in the wake of the fierce repressions following the assassination of Tsar Alexander II, the SPD became increasingly radicalised. Having regained legal status, it drew up and agreed in 1891 what is generally referred to as 'the Erfurt Programme'. Unlike the Gotha Programme, the Erfurt Programme was predicated on orthodox Marxist assumptions – but it fell short of calling for immediate revolution. It sought to appeal to both wings of the party. As the historian Carl E. Schorske explains:

> To the revolutionaries, the idealists, it said in effect, 'Patience! The time is not yet. Remember, history is on your side.' To the reformists ... it said, 'Reforms are the first task. Pursue them. But remember, you must fight for them.'
>
> (Schorske 1955: 6)

The deep ideological divisions within the party remained and gave rise to major ideological struggles. It was these struggles over revisionism, mass action and nationalism that refined Luxemburg's thinking, defined her as a significant theoretician and tactician and – above all – launched her as one of the most trenchant political activists and pamphleteers of her generation.

The struggle over revisionism

During the late 1890s, the economic situation in Germany was very different from the situation that had existed at the time of the Erfurt agreement. The SPD was now expanding not in an atmosphere of fierce repression and unemployment but in a period of economic expansion during which industrial production and wages had increased. So, the question arose: was the Erfurt Programme – a programme based on the conditions of misery and unemployment prevailing at the time – still relevant? Or was this the time to realign the SPD with an agenda that placed greater emphasis on parliamentary reform and less emphasis on the need for extra-parliamentary activity? Had the Erfurt Programme perhaps been a detour and was there now a need to return to the more reformist settlement established at Gotha in 1875? Or had the Gotha Programme – which had, after all, been subject to Marx's critical scrutiny in his 1875 *Critique of the Gotha Programme* – been a false start?

The chief protagonist on the reformist side of the argument was Eduard Bernstein, a German political journalist, who was 20 years older than Luxemburg and had joined the SPD the year after she was born. Returning from exile in London – where he had met and conversed with Engels and Lenin as well as with leading members of the recently formed Fabian Society – he was warmly received within the SPD as both a founding member of the party and as a self-made intellectual, who exercised considerable influence as an editor and writer. He was also a pacifist and, as Schorske describes him, 'a man of unimpeachable intellectual integrity' (1955: 16). In a series of articles published in *Leipziger Volkszeitung* ('*Leipzig People's Newspaper*') in September 1898 and 1899, he argued that, given there had been no world economic crisis for two decades, capitalism had developed a capacity for adjustment which would rule out economic crises in the future. He also noted a trend towards a more equitable distribution of wealth.

Bernstein spelled out his position in the Preface to his book *Evolutionary Socialism*, which was published in 1899 to coincide with the publication of his *Leipziger Volkszeitung* articles (see Bernstein 1961). The chief aim of his work, he argued, was 'to strengthen equally the realistic and the idealistic element in the socialist movement', but to do so 'by opposing what is left of the utopian mode of thought in the socialist theory' (Bernstein, 1961: xxxii). To adopt such a mode of thought – and here he takes a direct swipe at Luxemburg – may give rise to 'brilliant dialectical fireworks' but ends in 'smoke and mist' (Bernstein, 1961: 81). He argued that there was a national and evolutionary progression from 'liberalism as a great historical moment' to 'socialism as its legitimate heir' (Bernstein, 1961: 149) and rejected what he called 'the misery theory': 'the altogether outworn idea that the realisation of socialism depends on an increasing narrowing of the circle of the well-to-do and an increasing misery of the poor' (Bernstein, 1961: 175). Evoking the authority of the British Fabians, he claimed that '[n]o socialist capable of thinking, dreams today in England of an imminent victory for socialism by means of a violent revolution' (Bernstein, 1961: 203). Socialism, he concluded, could – and should – evolve through a process of adaptation and accommodation to a more benign and fair-minded capitalism.

Luxemburg's critique of Bernstein's articles was also published in the *Leipziger Volkszeitung*. After the publication of *Evolutionary*

Socialism, she followed this up with her 1899 pamphlet, *Social Reform or Revolution* (see R: 128–167). This built on her *Leipziger Volkszeitung* argument by providing a critique of Bernstein's book. She argued that the function of parliamentary reform was to prepare the groundwork for socialist revolution. The choice was not between reform and revolution, but between reform as an end in itself and reform as an element within a larger programme. 'Luxemburg insists', argues Helen Scott, 'that socialists cannot "counterpose" reform and revolution, but that rather there is an "indissoluble tie" between the two, the struggle for reforms being an essential means to the end of revolutionary transformation' (2010: 135). That transformation, Luxemburg argues, has to be undertaken within the context of a broader parliamentary and extra-parliamentary socialist movement. If reform activity is separated from that movement and thereby made an end in itself, then – as Luxemburg put it in her 1899 riposte to Bernstein – 'such activity not only does not lead to the realization of socialism as the ultimate goal, but moves in precisely the opposite direction' (R: 141).

She went on to argue that there could be no automatic transition from capitalism to socialism. Any such transition relies upon an increased understanding of the contradictions inherent in the capitalist economy:

> It is not true that socialism will arise automatically and under all circumstances from the daily struggle of the working class. Socialism will be the consequence only of the ever growing contradictions of capitalist economy and the comprehension by the working class of the unavoidability of the suppression of these contradictions through a social transformation.
>
> (R: 142)

The crucial question, she argues, is one of perspective: 'Bernstein's theory of adaptation is nothing but a theoretical generalization of the conception of the individual capitalist' (R: 145). He presents us with a view of capitalism 'as seen from the angle of the individual capitalist' (R: 145). This then allows Luxemburg, who has herself been accused of idealistic utopianism, to turn the table on Bernstein:

'it ends up with a reactionary and not a revolutionary program, and thus in a utopia' (R: 145).

In spite of Bernstein's timely intervention and the high regard in which he was generally held within the party, the SPD congress resolutions of 1899, 1901 and 1903 reaffirmed the Erfurt statement of principles and the idea of class struggle and rejected the position adopted by Bernstein and his fellow revisionists. Indeed, the Dresden resolution of September 1903, prompted in part by two years of recession and further success in the June elections of that year, was adamant in its condemnation of revisionism. In this instance, the SPD leadership aligned itself with the principles espoused by Luxemburg and the radical wing of the party. But from 1903, as the radicals began to push for action in support of those principles, the leadership adopted an increasingly reactionary stance on the major issues of the day, particularly, those relating to mass action and German nationalism.

The struggle over mass action

Throughout the boom years of 1895–1900, the trade unions had developed a tactic whereby workers tackled an industry not on a broad front but plant by plant. This tactic exploited the lack of unity among the employers within any given industry by attacking plants singly, while relying on the solidarity of the workers who contributed to a collective fund for those employed in whichever plant was on strike at any given time within their industry. Singly, employers were more or less powerless against this tactic, since the strike action would move from plant to plant as the employers gave in to the demands of the workers. However, as the employers began to form employers' associations, they developed their own counter-tactics, chief among which was the mass lockout aimed at exhausting the union funds available to support the strikers. The collective action of the workers was thereby matched by the collective determination of the employers to starve them out. By the time of the recession of 1900–1902, the use of limited strike action undertaken for limited gain within a particular industry was giving way to the idea of mass strike action undertaken across industries and for the purpose of bringing about radical economic and social change.

Rosa Luxemburg played a crucial role in articulating this shift. She was a close observer of the April 1902 Belgian general strike for universal, equal suffrage and later that year published a stinging attack – titled *A Tactical Question* – on the Belgian Social Democrats for having agreed to drop their call for women's suffrage at the demand of the Liberals with whom they were in electoral coalition (see R: 233–236). The strike was lost, she argued, because of parliamentary expediency and the failure of the labour leaders to support mass action. In 1903, she was asked by the editors of *Iskra* ('*Spark*'), a Menshevik-dominated journal, to analyse the split between the Mensheviks and the Bolsheviks in the Russian Social Democratic Party. In the following year, 1904, she published her analysis, *Organisational Questions of Russian Social Democracy*, in the theoretical journal of the SPD, *Die Neue Zeit* ('*The New Times*') (see R: 248–265). Again, her analysis focused on the political potential of mass action and the failure of leadership to realize that potential, but on this occasion, her critique was aimed not at the Belgian Social Democrats but at Lenin.

She accused Lenin of 'uncompromising centralism', arguing that by imposing upon local party organisations 'the strict discipline and the direct, decisive and definite intervention of the central authority' he was wrenching 'active revolutionaries from their, albeit unorganized, revolutionary activist milieu' (R: 250). 'His line of thought,' she argued, 'is concerned principally with the control of party activity and not with its fertilization, with *narrowing* and not with *broadening*, with *tying the movement up* and not with *drawing it together*.' (R: 256, emphasis in original). She argued for 'a completely new notion of the mutual relationship between organization and struggle' (R: 251), whereby the organisation of collective action is achieved through the raised consciousness of those actively engaged in the struggle. She argued,

Organisation, enlightenment and struggle are here not separate moments mechanically divided in time … [T]hey are merely different facets of the same process … [T]here is no ready-made predetermined and detailed tactic of struggle that the Central Committee could drill into the social democratic membership.

(R: 252)

In spite of Luxemburg's criticism of Lenin, she worked closely with him throughout the rest of her life, particularly in the aftermath of the 1905 Revolution. But the differences between them on matters relating to organisation and leadership were stark and – for Luxemburg if not for Lenin – gained increasing significance.

Luxemburg was developing these insights into the nature of collective action at a time of immense personal struggle. In January 1904, a regional court in the state of Saxony convicted her of 'lese majesty' for allegedly insulting the Prussian monarch, William II, in one of her campaign speeches delivered the previous year. In July, following an unsuccessful appeal against the conviction, the court sentenced her to three months in prison. She began serving her sentence in August, but was given early release in October as part of a general amnesty to mark the coronation of the new King of Saxony, Frederick Augustus III. Jogiches was still very much part of her life, but she was becoming less dependent upon him and increasingly reliant on her close female friends for emotional support and for the sharing of day-to-day concerns. Jogiches was unable to give her the sense of emotional security that she craved.

In spite of the turmoil and uncertainty regarding the protracted conviction, appeal and sentencing process, Luxemburg seems on this occasion to have found the experience of imprisonment strangely restorative. Writing to one of her close female friends, Luise Kautsky, in a letter dated September 1904, she observed through the window of her cell that '[o]utdoors a horse is being led slowly past the prison on its way home and in the nocturnal stillness the clopping of its hoofs on the pavement resounds in an oddly peaceful way' (L: 175). Prison allowed her the time and, ironically, the space to relinquish her role as participant and adopt that of spectator. 'Life plays an eternal game of tag with me,' she wrote in that same letter Luise Kautsky, 'It seems to me always that it's not inside me, not here where I am, but somewhere far off' (L: 175).

The struggle over mass action was still high on the political agenda when Luxemburg was released from prison. A wave of mass political and social unrest was spreading through vast areas of the Russian Empire and Russian-partitioned Poland involving worker strikes, peasant unrest and military mutiny. In January 1905, this culminated in Bloody Sunday in St Petersburg, when unarmed demonstrators were fired upon by soldiers of the Imperial Guard as they marched towards the Winter Palace to present a petition to Tsar Nicholas II of Russia. Germany, too, was in the grip of a series of intense labour struggles, the first and greatest of which was the coal strike in the Ruhr basin, which lasted from January to early February 1905. In July, Luxemburg visited Jogiches for four weeks in Cracow, where he had gone to organise activities within the Social Democracy and the Kingdom of Poland (SDKP) party, which she and Jogiches had helped form a decade earlier. In September, she returned to Cracow, but in between these two visits was the hugely important annual SPD party congress, which occasioned a head-on clash between the radical wing of the party and the trade union leaders.

The Jena congress was convened on 17 September 1905. Prior to the congress, union leaders had met in Cologne in May of that year and unreservedly opposed the notion of a general strike. In doing so, they were setting themselves against the radical wing of the party and in effect warning its leadership not to back the case for mass action at the forthcoming Jena congress. At the congress, Luxemburg led the radical wing in calling on the SPD to adopt a strategy of mass strike action. The co-chair of the SPD, August Ferdinand Bebel, proposed by way of compromise that the mass strike should be seen as a defensive measure of last resort that allowed for the possibility of a mass strike but distinguished it from revolutionary action. Bebel's mass strike resolution was accepted by congress and – in spite of its many qualifications – was interpreted by the radical wing as a sign of the SPD's capacity for revolutionary development. The party had, they maintained, quite clearly rejected the position taken by the trade unions at its Köln congress.

Following the Jena congress, Luxemburg returned to Cracow and from there, moved to Warsaw to participate in the June uprising by the Polish workers in Łódź against the Russian Empire. Arriving too late to participate fully in the uprising, she and Jogiches were nevertheless arrested in Warsaw in March 1906. Luxemburg was released in the following July on health grounds, but Jogiches remained in custody. Her health had undoubtedly suffered from the conditions in the prison and from her own participation in a six-day hunger strike, but her early release was also due to pressure exerted on her behalf by social democrats in Germany and Poland. In August, she made her way to Finland where she had extensive discussions on the subject of the mass strike with Lenin and his immediate Bolshevik circle. While in Finland, she wrote *The Mass Strike, the Political Party, and the Trade Unions*[1] at the invitation of the Social Democratic organisation in Hamburg (see R: 168–199).[2] The pamphlet was published in autumn 1906 and – along with her earlier pamphlet, *Social Reform or Revolution* – stands as one of the great political pamphlets of that period.

The Mass Strike focuses on the revolutionary potential of mass action. The first part of the pamphlet provides a brief history of the mass strike in Russia, while the second part draws out four implications from this history. First, she argues that: '[i]t is absurd to think of the mass strike as one act, one isolated action. The mass strike is rather the indication, the rallying idea, of a whole period of the class struggle lasting for years, perhaps for decades' (R: 192). Second, she argues that 'it is impossible to separate the economic and the political factors from one another' (R: 194). Third, she claims that 'the mass strike is inseparable from the revolution' (R: 195). The revolution, in other words, is a process as well as an event. Moreover, it is a process that is determined by the interaction of economic and political factors. It cannot be reduced to a set of economic demands.

Finally, she insists that 'the mass strike cannot be called at will, even when the decision to do so may come from the highest committee of the strongest Social Democratic party' (R: 197): there must be 'an element of spontaneity' (R: 198). But just as there is a synergy between the economic and the political in Luxemburg's notion of the mass strike, so there is a synergy between spontaneity and organisation in her notion of revolution. She is not arguing against organisation as such, but against any kind of organisation that is imposed from above or from outside the arena of collective action. 'Instead of puzzling their heads with the technical side, with the mechanism of the mass strike, the Social Democrats are called upon to assume *political* leadership in the midst of the revolutionary period' (R: 199, emphasis in original). For Luxemburg, organisation must crystallise around the collective will of those actively engaged in the struggle. 'Correctly understood,' as Norman Geras argues with regard to Luxemburg's thinking on the mass strike, 'the political and tactical conceptions at the heart of it lead away from spontaneism and economism' ([1976] 2015: 126).

From Finland, she returned to Germany to participate in the annual SPD congress, which on this occasion was held in Mannheim in September 1906. Prior to the conference, in the previous February, the trade union leaders and the SPD executive had met with a view to securing cooperation on the mass strike question. The radical wing of the party had not only been excluded from this meeting, but had been given no information regarding its outcomes. At issue was the control of strike action. The unions argued that such action came under their control and their control alone. The radicals, on the other hand, argued that the trade unions were subordinate to the decisions of the party and must be bound by them. The party executive sought a compromise position whereby the trade unions would agree to act in the spirit of the SPD, while omitting any mention of the trade unions being bound by the decisions of the party. The compromise resolution was passed thereby severely limiting the possibility of party support of mass political action.

As Schorske writes,

> The Mannheim resolution was a landmark in the history of German Social Democracy. It represented a kind of counter-revolution in the party, a reversal of the radical victory at the battle of Jena the previous year.
>
> (Schorske 1955: 51)

Luxemburg's pamphlet had clearly failed in its immediate purpose of gaining the backing of the party for mass political action. In the aftermath of the conference, she wrote to her great friend Clara

Zetkin, a leading activist and theorist in the German women's movement:

> The situation is simply this: August [Bebel], and the others even more so, have given themselves over entirely to parliamentarism and *for* parliamentarism. They will totally renounce any turn of events that goes beyond the limits of parliamentarism; indeed, they will go further, seeking to push and twist everything back into the parliamentary mold ... The masses, and still more the great mass of [party] *comrades*, in their heart of hearts have had their fill of parliamentarism. That's the feeling I get.
>
> (L: 237, emphasis in original)

In December, she stood trial yet again, this time for remarks made at the SPD congress in Jena in the previous year. She was sentenced to two months imprisonment for alleged 'incitement to acts of violence' due to begin the following summer.

The struggle over nationalism

As always with Luxemburg, life history, European history and world history were intricately interwoven with the history of the SPD. Several months after her return to Germany – probably around April 1907 – she began an intimate relationship with Konstantin (or Kostya) Zetkin, who was 14 years younger than her. Kostya Zetkin was the son of her great friend and fellow radical Clara Zetkin, who, as far as we known, was not aware of the relationship. The precise details regarding the whereabouts of Jogiches at this time are obscure. Having been sentenced in January 1907 to eight years' hard labour in Siberia, he escaped in February and lived in hiding for a short time in Warsaw, and then in Cracow, before travelling through to Germany in April on the way to London for the Russian Social Democratic Workers' Party (RSDRP) congress in London in May of that year.

Believing that Jogiches was involved with another woman in the Polish Socialist Party (PPS), Luxemburg had already broken off relations with him. However, she was due to address the RSDRP conference so their paths inevitably crossed. Their brief time together in London was highly fraught and mutually recriminatory. Sexual jealousy no doubt played its part, but Luxemburg had undoubtedly had enough of a relationship that was at once hugely demanding and at the same time emotionally unfulfilling. The prospect of a more relaxed relationship with Zetkin was no doubt a welcome change from the intensity and uncertainty of her relationship with Jogiches. (Her hand-drawn sketches of Zetkin – depicting him physically relaxed, asleep or deep in thought – are in stark contrast to the impression she gives in her letters of Jogiches as forever restless and fuelled by nervous energy) (see illustrations included in L: 292–293).

Nationalism – along with the continuing struggle over revisionism and mass action – had by this time become a major focus for disagreement within the SPD. Luxemburg had already begun to work out her position on this issue. She had used the opportunity afforded by the 1893 congress of the Second International Congress in Zurich to distance herself from the PPS and argue against Polish independence. Indeed this had been one of the main justifications for the founding of the Social Democracy and the Kingdom of Poland (SDKP) party as a breakaway from PPS. She had also, in 1900, defended the right of schoolchildren in Posen (now Poznań) to be taught religion in Polish. At the time, German became the sole language in government offices and law courts, and the use of the Polish language was prohibited in municipal council debates; many place names and family names were Germanised. These two positions – against Polish independence and pro-mother tongue – may seem contradictory but Luxemburg's point was that the workers of Poland and Germany had more in common with each other than they had with the ruling elites of either nationality. Thus, as she expressed it,

we must not march behind them these land-owners and bourgeois, but *against* them; we must not seek our salvation for our nationality in company with them, but look to defend both our livelihoods and our mother tongue *in conflict* with them.

(S: 47–48)

The national question gained international significance with the Moroccan crisis of 1905, when Kaiser Wilhelm of Germany attempted to disrupt the Anglo-French Entente ('Entente Cordiale') between Britain and France. By the terms of this agreement, Britain could pursue its interests in Egypt, while France was free to expand westward from Algeria to Morocco. France subsequently signed an agreement with Spain dividing Morocco into spheres of influence, with France receiving the lion's share. Wilhelm travelled to Tangiers and on arrival declared his support for the sultan as overall ruler of Morocco, with no obligations to foreign powers. He further announced that he would negotiate with the sultan directly on all matters rather than through foreign intermediaries and that he expected Germany to have the same advantages in trade and commerce as those enjoyed by other countries. Although Wilhelm's intention had been to drive a wedge between Britain and France, his intervention had the effect of uniting them in defence against what they perceived to be an aggressive or at the very least a provocative act. The Anglo-French Entente was thereby strengthened rather than weakened by the German challenge to France and had the further unintended consequence of driving Russia into a mutual defence agreement with Britain and France. Germany had inadvertently – and spectacularly – isolated itself. Christopher Clark's blunt judgement seems about right: 'The German policy makers had bungled' (2013: 157).

It was the radical left grouping within the SPD that grasped the dangers inherent in the militaristic nationalism that was now gripping the country. The SPD had suffered grave electoral setbacks in the January elections; its number of seats in the Reichstag dropping from 81 to 43. This electoral defeat had immediate repercussions on the SPD's official attitude towards national debates on military issues and foreign affairs. Bebel, as co-chair of the party, was particularly anxious to avoid any suggestion that the party was unpatriotic. As a result, he vehemently opposed the anti-militarist arguments of, among others, Karl Liebknecht and Rosa Luxemburg. Liebknecht had called for determined anti-militarist agitation at successive party congresses and in February published a tract titled *Militarism and Anti-Militarism* (see Liebknecht, [1907] 2012). In it, he argued that '[m]ilitarism ... expresses in the strongest, most concentrated and exclusive form the national, cultural, and class instinct of self-preservation' (Liebknecht, [1907] 2012: 13) and that anti-militarism had been a central plank of the Second International since its inception. 'The power to lessen the number of wars by means of agitating and by enlightening the nations,' asserted Liebknecht, 'is ascribed to the labour organizations, and it is laid down as a duty to work indefatigably with this end in view' (Liebknecht, [1907] 2012: 87–88). In other words, the SPD was out of step with the onward march of the Second International.

After the publication of *Militarism and Anti-Militarism*, Liebknecht was arrested and imprisoned for eighteen months, in spite of which he was elected to parliament the following year while still in jail. The dispute within the SPD came to a head in the Reichstag debate on the military budget in April 1907. Bebel attacked the abuses of German militarism with examples of the brutal treatment of soldiers and harsh military justice, but tempered this critique of militarism by arguing that it impaired the quality of the German army. However, Gustav Noske, who was to have a major part to play in Luxemburg's murder, devoted his first major speech in the Reichstag to distancing himself and the SPD entirely and unequivocally from the anti-militarists within the party. The stance adopted by Noske during this debate on the military budget incited fierce dispute throughout the party and more widely within the Second International.

Luxemburg travelled to London in the last two weeks of May 1907 in order to participate in the fifth congress of the RSDRP. Her *Address to the Fifth Congress of the Russian Social Democratic Labor Party* was given at a session chaired by Lenin (see R: 200–207.) Building on some of the major themes developed in her 1899 *Social Reform or Revolution*, her 1904 *Organisational Questions of Russian Social Democracy*, and her 1906 *The Mass Strike*, she called for an international unification of the Labour movement under the auspices of the SPD: 'not just a formal, purely mechanical unity, but an inner cohesion, an inner strength which genuinely will result from clear, correct tactics corresponding to this inner unity of the class struggle of the proletariat' (R: 207). Luxemburg's visit to London proved a grim experience. Not only did she endure a bruising encounter with Jogiches, but she also found her immediate surroundings gloomy and alienating. Moreover, she felt that the party congress was failing to build on what she saw as the achievements of the 1905 Revolution. Writing to Kostya Zetkin, in a letter dated 13 May 1907, she tried to explain her sense of alienation:

> I'm sitting in the middle of the famous Whitechapel district … In a foul mood I travelled through the endless stations of the dark Underground and emerged both depressed and lost in a strange and wild part of the city.
>
> (L: 239)

Having served her two-month prison sentence in June and July – as pronounced in December of the previous year – Luxemburg attended the Socialist International Congress in Stuttgart in August 1907. She stayed with her friend Clara Zetkin, whom she introduced to Lenin, and the three of them spent much of the congress in conversation with one another. Supported by Lenin, whose position on this matter was similar to her own, Luxemburg addressed the congress in the name of the Polish and Russian delegations, arguing that the struggle against militarism cannot be separated from the class war. The SPD was fiercely divided. The German delegation cast its entire block vote against a motion affirming the absolute hostility of the International to colonialism. The motion – supported by Lenin and Luxemburg – was nevertheless carried. The radicals had won the argument within the forum of the Second International, but in doing so had become completely isolated within the SPD. Following the Stuttgart congress, the SPD became the leading conservative force within the International.

In September, the divisions within the party exploded at the SPD congress held at Essen. Luxemburg and her fellow anti-militarists were singled out for vilification by those who declared complete satisfaction with the positions of Noske and Bebel. Noske in particular dominated the debate, drawing support from those who favoured an exclusively parliamentary tactic as opposed to those who located the political struggle within a broader spectrum of collective action. Having finally cut loose from her intimate relations with Jogiches and set herself firmly against the mainstream of the SPD, Luxemburg was finding her way through to what she described, in a letter to Kostya Zetkin dated 24 September 1907, as 'a calm, regular life and diligent work'. Addressing Zetkin as 'Sweet little beloved', she tells him: 'Finally I am back in line with [the work I want to do on] economics. I had gotten completely out of the habit of [systematic or intensive] thinking, and that depressed me greatly' (L: 245). She was about to embark on the last and most intellectually creative decade of her life.

THE YEARS OF CONSOLIDATION

Luxemburg's return to economics was to extend and deepen the analysis she had developed in her doctoral study and also to strengthen the political arguments she had been advancing in her major pamphlets and speeches. She had, by this time, become a recognised authority within the Second International on Polish and Russian affairs. The further work she was to undertake on capital accumulation enabled her to gather her earlier arguments and analyses into an economic theory of global exploitation. It thereby transformed her from a remarkable political activist and pamphleteer operating on the radical wing of the SPD to a politically engaged intellectual, committed to the struggle against capitalist exploitation and imperial expansionism. The political activist was still alive and kicking, but would increasingly operate within a broader and more clearly defined sense of political purpose. The years between 1908 and the outbreak of the First World War – when Luxemburg was between 37 and 43 years of age – were not without their strife and conflict, but were in the main a period of consolidation. It was a time of *reculer pour mieux sauter*: a period of drawing back, of gathering and taking stock, in order to make the final leap into revolutionary action.

In 1906, the SPD had established a Party School in Berlin. Every winter up to the outbreak of First World War, about 30 party and trade union members, chosen by their district organisations, attended the school. Luxemburg was engaged from 1907 and was assigned the course on economics. The school provided her with a regular and steady income of 3,600 marks per course, which was a considerable sum. While the school was in session, she lectured for two hours each morning with extra time devoted to students and colleagues during the afternoon. Her students came from a variety of backgrounds and regions and covered a wide age range. According to Frölich, '[s]he proved an outstanding teacher ... She never lectured at them and promised no ready-made answers, compelling them to work out their own ideas and conclusions' ([1939] 2010: 146–147). He adds: 'Their work with her brought Rosa Luxemburg's pupils not only an intellectual gain but a moral awakening' ([1939] 2010: 148). She clearly had the capacity to explain and clarify complicated economic and philosophical issues and to relate these to the particular circumstances of her students.

The Party School was not without its critics. There were two main lines of critical argument: the first held that the school was there to help raise the general level of education among workers and that it was failing to do so; the second that it should be a kind of training college for SPD activists and that again, it was not fulfilling this task. Luxemburg was asked by the SPD executive to defend the school against these criticisms at the 1908 party congress held in Nurnberg. She delivered a measured defence conceding that there was room for improvement, but arguing against the introduction of either an over-generalised curriculum that would in her view offer a smattering of unrelated ideas and information or a training programme focusing primarily on the kinds of contextual and organisational issues with which many of the students were in her view already well acquainted. Her point was that the tactical know-how associated with practical reasoning goes hand in hand with the conceptual clarity associated with theoretical understanding. She also pointed out that the students would go on learning all their lives and that the school needed to provide a resource that would inform and enhance their lifelong learning and ground it in an understanding of how – from a Marxist perspective – the political economy works.

Luxemburg's lectures for the SPD School in Berlin formed the basis of an unfinished book *Introduction to Political Economy*, which she worked on from 1908 (see CW I: 89–300). Her work on the *Introduction* allowed her to clarify her general approach as a political economist, while positioning herself within and against the academic field of political economy as it then existed. Historical analysis provided her with a perspective from which to view both the capitalist mode of production and the work of earlier political economists in grasping and elucidating the laws by which capitalism operates. Political economy had, she argued, evolved alongside capitalism and had therefore examined it on its own terms and according to its own presuppositions. As a result, it had failed to grasp the relation between capitalism and global exploitation or to grapple with the historicity of capitalism as an economic system. Luxemburg was intent upon exposing the limitations of 'present-day political economy', which she saw as nothing more than 'a scientific mystification in the interest of the bourgeoisie' (CW I: 122): only when the 'present-day political economy' had been exposed as an apologia for capitalism, could economic analysis become 'a weapon of the revolutionary class struggle for the liberation of the proletariat' (CW I: 141).

During the summer of 1909, Luxemburg visited Italy, spending time in Zurich on both her outward and return journeys. On her return to Berlin, she attempted to end her relationship with Kostya Zetkin. Kostya was 14 years younger than her and the son of her best friend. She sensed that, in spite of their mutual tenderness and intimacy, he felt constrained. So, she took responsibility for ending the relationship. In a letter dated 17 August, 1909 – which, as she put it, 'costs me great effort of will' – she freed him of any responsibility he might feel towards her: 'Now you are free as a bird, and may you be happy ... Fare thee well, and may the nightingales of the Apennine Hills sing to you and the wide-horned oxen of the Caucasus greet you' (L: 286). Her farewell to Kostya reveals something of Luxemburg's capacity for self-dramatisation, but it also shows her sensitivity and generosity to a younger man, who clearly loved her but may have felt trapped in a relationship with an older, stronger woman, who was also a close friend and confidante of his mother, Clara Zetkin. The relationship, in fact, continued for some time with Kostya torn between the desire for independence and his need for Luxemburg. By the outbreak of the First World War, however, their relationship had almost certainly matured into a platonic friendship.

The first three months of 1910 saw a powerful upsurge of struggle by the German working class – including strikes, demonstrations and clashes with police – to end the Prussian three-class voting system and press for general suffrage. Only men over the age of 24 were allowed to vote and then according to a system whereby the electorate was divided into three classes calculated according to how much tax one paid. The poorest constituted by far the largest class numerically, but elected only a third of the representatives. The vote of a wealthy tax-paying male was, in other words, worth significantly more than the vote of a poor tax-paying person. In March, Luxemburg submitted an article titled 'What Next?' to SPD journal *Vorwärts*. In this article, she urged official encouragement from the party for demonstration strikes and for a general discussion of the mass strike as a form of collective political action. The editors rejected Luxemburg's article on the grounds that the party instructions forbade them from printing propaganda for the mass strikes. Karl Kautsky, a leading theorist within the SPD and co-founder and chief editor of *Neue Zeit*, similarly turned the piece down. The two chief organs of the SPD – *Vorwärts* and *Neue Zeit* – had both in effect censored a major radical voice within the party. Moreover, they did so not on the basis of a considered judgement regarding the merit of the article but on the grounds that it contravened party policy.

This marked a decisive break between Luxemburg and Kautsky, who had provided her with considerable support since her arrival in Berlin and whose wife, Luise Kautsky, was a close and lifelong friend. Kautsky took issue with Luxemburg in an article titled 'What Now?', which he published in *Neue Zeit* and in which he argued that the time was not ripe for struggles outside the electoral, parliamentary arena. He claimed that the comparisons with Russia in 1905 were not valid, that the situation in Germany where political and civil rights had already been won was very different, and that any call for mass action was at best premature. Kautsky was pointing to a middle way between the revisionists – against whom he had, with Luxemburg and others, taken issue – and the radical wing of the party led by Luxemburg and others from which he now publically distanced himself. At issue was whether to toe the parliamentary line or to employ – in addition to parliamentary reform – extra-parliamentary means of collective action. In his exchange with Luxemburg, Kautsky distanced himself from any position that lent weight to extra-parliamentary action as opposed to legal-parliamentary action, while Luxemburg declared emphatically that extra-parliamentary action was a political necessity.

Luxemburg responded publicly to Kautsky in the pages of *Neue Zeit*. Her article was titled 'Theory and Practice' and was a thorough, reasoned but highly polemical riposte to Kautsky's position, as outlined in his previous 'What Now?' paper (see R: 208–231). She opened the article in characteristically combative mode: 'The first question which the interest of party circles demands in our present dispute is this: whether discussion of the mass strike was obstructed in the party press, namely in *Vorwärts* and *Neue Zeit*' (R: 208). She challenged Kautsky's depiction of the Russian situation, which, she claimed, 'is, in most important points, an almost total reversal of the truth' (R: 216). She argued that the Russian peasants did not begin to rebel in 1905, as Kautsky suggested, but that 'peasant uprisings run like a red thread through the internal history of Russia; uprisings against the landowners as well as violent resistance to the organs of government' (R: 208). Moreover, to claim, as Kautsky had done, that the mass strike actions of the Russian proletariat were chaotic affairs, born out of bewilderment was 'a blooming fantasy'. Nothing could be further from the truth. Mass action had succeeded in 'abolishing piecework, household work, night work, factory penalties, and of forcing strict observance of Sundays off' (R: 217).

Having attacked the factual basis of Kautsky's argument, she proceeded to challenge his underlying assumptions. These, she argued, constituted a fundamental misrepresentation of the history of the socialist struggle and a consequent misrepresentation of the German proletariat. The part played by the political mass strike in the Russian Revolution was not, as Kautsky had claimed, 'a product of Russia's economic and political *backwardness*' (R: 222, emphasis in original). On the contrary, the Russian Revolution had revealed the political mass strike to be highly effective and the Russian proletariat to be in the vanguard of revolutionary action. Returning to the unresolved issues so fiercely debated at the party congress of 1905, Luxemburg insisted that Kautsky was flouting 'the spirit of the Russian revolution' and that in doing so, he was proposing 'a frightfully fundamental revision of the Jena resolution' (R: 224). She repeatedly asserts that Kautsky writes as a theorist and that his most recent arguments are yet another example of theory becoming disconnected from the reality of labour history and the history of the socialist struggle. Kautsky was, from Luxemburg's perspective, giving theoretical cover to revisionists within the party. 'It seems,' she remarks in polemical mode, 'that "theory" does not merely "stride forward" more slowly than practice: alas, from time to time it also goes tumbling backwards' (R: 222).

It is striking, as Massimo Salvadori points out, that Kautsky, who had constantly warned against revisionism and the dangers of bureaucratisation, seems not to have grasped what Luxemburg had understood and articulated with such clarity: 'that a cleavage was arising between a "goal" that was socialist and a "means" that was ever more thoroughly administered by a conservative and moderate bureaucracy, which was now concerned to fortify the organization solely within the dominant system' (1990: 144). If, as a result of this historic exchange, Kautsky had defined himself as a centrist, positioned between the radical wing of the party and the revisionists, Luxemburg had made a very public declaration of her unwavering support for the radical wing. The 1911 congress in Magdeburg was the last party congress at which a defence against revisionism was the central item on the agenda. Kautsky, who was suffering from exhaustion and whose marriage to Luise Kautsky was under considerable strain, did not attend. Luxemburg, who did attend, was politically outflanked and personally isolated. The personal isolation was compounded by the suspicion that her close friendship with Luise Kautsky had contributed to tensions within the Kautsky household.

The SPD now comprised a number of clearly defined positions: an increasingly vulnerable radical wing in support of extra-parliamentary action in addition to parliamentary action; a moderate wing in support of legal-parliamentary action; and a revisionist wing increasingly antagonistic towards any form of extra-parliamentary action. This triad of positions defined the fate of the SPD. It identified Luxemburg as one of the key protagonists of the radical wing of the party, Kautsky as an increasingly influential spokesperson of the centre, and Noske as a leading figure within the increasingly conservative-inclined revisionist wing. It also defined the course of

German and European history, leading to what Schorske (1955) termed 'the great schism': the rift between those on the radical, anti-militarist wing of the party who opposed the build-up to what was to become the First World War and those on the increasingly powerful right wing who supported it. It was a fatal schism that was to result in Luxemburg's imprisonment four years later and Noske's collusion in – and at least partial responsibility for – her brutal murder in the aftermath of war.

Notwithstanding her increasing isolations and misgivings, Luxemburg refused to split from the party. She pressed ahead with her teaching in the Party School, her extensive correspondence with friends and party associates, her speaking engagements, and above all, her continuing work on the theory and practice of economic reproduction. The latter gained renewed impetus when in November 1911 she came across an unexpected difficulty while working on her *Introduction to Political Economy*. The difficulty related to Marx's explanation of capitalist accumulation, as occurring within a closed capitalist society without foreign trade. Luxemburg became increasingly convinced that capitalist development depends upon the existence of non-capitalist areas, which act as a provider of both commodity outlets and inputs such as raw materials and labour. What she took to be the inadequacy of Marx's explanation led her to an insight that was to have a profound impact on her own thinking: capitalism cannot be explained according to static and national economic models, but only in terms of dynamic exploitative relationships between capitalist economies and peripheral economies.

This insight led Luxemburg to temporarily abandon work on the *Introduction to Political Economy* and embark on what is now generally considered to be her *magnum opus*: *The Accumulation of Capital: A Contribution to the Economic Theory of Imperialism* (see CW II: 1–342). Working under great pressure, she completed the book in 12 months, that is, by the end of 1912. In it, she attempted to uncover the economic roots of imperialism. Capitalism, she argued, is required by its very nature to dominate and exploit whatever remains of the non-capitalist world in pursuit of raw materials and potential markets. When it has exhausted the world's resources, it will, she further argued, collapse into barbarism unless alternatives are in place.

The final victory of socialism over capitalism is not, she insisted, an historical necessity: there is nothing inevitable about the dawn of socialism. To think otherwise is to indulge in naive utopianism.

Following the publication of *The Accumulation of Capital* in 1913, the paramount question for Luxemburg was therefore how to identify and put in place – in the here and now – the social and economic conditions necessary for a genuinely democratic and socialist post-capitalist and post-imperialist world. 'The history of socialism is the school of life', she had declared in a speech she had delivered in 1908 (quoted in Scott 2008: 30). And in her case, it most certainly was. She had served her apprenticeship. It was now time to enter history – through the passageway of prolonged imprisonment.

2

Entering History

PROTECTIVE CUSTODY

On 4 August 1914, the parliamentary membership of the SPD voted in favour of providing economic support – 'war credits' – for what was rapidly developing into a major European conflagration. It was a watershed moment for Luxemburg, the SPD and the Second International. It brought Luxemburg to the edge of despair and the radical wing of the SPD to an embarrassing capitulation. It also heralded the end of the Second International. In hindsight, it is possible to see how the very few radicals within the SPD membership of the Reichstag were wrong-footed by the escalating and wholly unpredictable rush of events that followed the assassination of Archduke Franz Ferdinand in Sarajevo on 28 June: the declaration of war on Serbia by Austria-Hungary on 28 July; the declaration of war on Russia by Germany on 31 July; the invasion of Luxembourg by Germany on 2 August; the declaration of war on France by Germany and the invasion of Belgium by Germany on 3 August; and the declaration of war on Germany by the UK on 4 August. By the time the crucial vote on war credits was called, war was inevitable and conflicting loyalties and priorities were stretched to breaking point

Luxemburg immediately grasped the enormity of the situation. Writing in November 1914 to her lover and friend, Hans Diefenbach, who had been conscripted into the German army, she remarked upon the historic nature of the events that were unfolding:

> That the party [the SPD] and the International have gone kaput, thoroughly kaput, is not open to any doubt, but precisely the increasing dimensions of the disaster have made of it a world-historical drama, and in this regard the objective historical significance comes to the fore.

(L: 337)

She continued to agitate and pamphleteer against the war, but had a prison sentence hanging over her: a sentence deferred from February 1914, when in Frankfurt she was sentenced to one year's imprisonment for inciting soldiers to disobedience in a speech delivered in September of the previous year. Because of pending appeal procedures and Luxemburg's evident ill health, her imprisonment was deferred – supposedly until 1 March 1915, although in the event, she was brought to the women's prison in Barnimstrasse in Berlin on 19 February 1915.

She was released from prison in early 1916, by which time she had drafted two major works: a response to her critics titled *The Accumulation of Capital, Or, What the Epigones have Made of Marx's Theory – An Anti-Critique*,[1] which was first published in 1921, and her pseudonymous *The Junius Pamphlet: The Crisis of German Social Democracy*,[2] which had been smuggled out of prison and was first published in 1916 as a pamphlet in Zurich (see CW II: 343–449; R: 312–341). In the latter, she argued that what united the working class of all sides was greater than – but also diametrically opposed to – the partisan and nationalist loyalties that divided them, namely, their shared experience of exploitation by nation states committed to imperialist expansion. She further argued that the state was one of the main vehicles of capitalist exploitation and called for an international coalition of resistance involving workers from all sides of an increasingly complex nexus of alliances and counter-alliances.

The ideas contained in *The Junius Pamphlet* became the basis of the perspective adopted by the International Group (or Spartacus Group – named after the leader of the largest slave rebellion in ancient Rome), which was first formed in August 1916 with a core group comprising, among others, Jogiches, Liebknecht, Luxemburg, Mehring and Zetkin. In the wake of an intense propaganda campaign mounted by the International Group, Liebknecht was sentenced on 28 June 2016 to two years and six months hard labour – later increased by a higher military court to four years. Demonstrations and strikes were mounted in support of Liebknecht, but these were repressed and mass trials and severe sentencing followed. After an unsuccessful appeal, Liebknecht began his prison sentence on 6 December 1916.

By this time, Luxemburg had been re-arrested under a 'protective custody' order, which took effect on 10 July 1916. Again, she was brought to the women's prison in Barnimstrasse in Berlin, where as a political prisoner she was allowed considerable personal freedom, but was given no indication of when her period of custody would come to an end. Under a 'protective custody' warrant, no prisoner could be held for more than three months, but this simply meant that new arrest warrants were issued every three months with no restriction on the number of warrants issued. At the end of October 1916, she was transferred to the fortress prison of Wronke situated in western-central Poland. Again, conditions were not unduly restrictive. Her cell door was left open all day and she was allowed to tend her flower beds in the prison yard and pursue both her botanical and ornithological interests. But her term of imprisonment remained in effect open-ended and entirely at the whim of the state. She could only wait. But in her case – as in the case of all political prisoners – the waiting involved immense and chronic uncertainty.

Throughout her period of imprisonment, she smuggled out a constant stream of articles and letters to fellow activists, while also keeping up a regular correspondence with a wide network of friends and fellow activists. Never naively optimistic – and throughout her life periodically overcome by fierce bouts of depression – she nevertheless clung to the notion of 'joy' as a kind of ethical imperative. In a letter dated 28 December 1916 and addressed to her friend Mathilde Wurm, she wrote:

> To be a human being is the main thing, above all else. And that means: to be firm and clear and **cheerful**, yes, cheerful in spite of everything and anything … To be a human being means joyfully to toss your entire life 'on the giant scales of fates' if it must be so, and at the same time to rejoice in the brightness of everyday and the beauty of every cloud … The world is so beautiful, with all its horrors.
>
> (L: 363, emphasis in original)

Luxemburg's letters during this period bear testimony to her immensely complex and multifaceted personality. Writing sometime after her death, Walter Benjamin – himself an extremely complicated character – recorded how he was 'deeply moved by [the] unbelievable beauty and significance' of her letters from prison (quoted in Eiland and Jennings 2014: 127). The sheer volume of her letters and her range of correspondents reveal a tremendous capacity for friendship. Many of them also express her own sense of vulnerability, which she sees reflected in the vulnerability of nature. Writing in March 1917, she tells Diefenbach about her day ('another grey day, without sun – a cold east wind'):

> I feel like a frozen bumblebee; have you ever found a bumblebee like that in the garden after the first frosty morning, lying on its back quite cold and still as though dead, lying in the grass with its little legs drawn in and its little fur coat with hoarfrost? … I always made it my business to kneel down next to such a frozen bumblebee and waken it back to life by blowing on it with my warm breath.
>
> (L: 384–385)

In July 1917, she was uprooted yet again – this time to Breslau (now Wrocław) in west Poland. She remained tireless in maintaining her correspondence with friends and fellow workers in the SPD and the wider Second International. She rarely slips into self-absorbed monologues, but engages with her correspondents on their own terms in what constitutes an ongoing conversation. Writing in August 1917 to Sophie Liebknecht (husband of Karl Liebknecht), Luxemburg engages directly with her friend's concerns regarding the incarceration of her husband and her own state of mind:

> You ask 'How does one become good?' … Sonyichka, I don't know any way other than to link up with the cheerfulness and beauty of life which are always around us everywhere, if only one knows how to use one's eyes and ears, and thus to create an inner equilibrium and rise above everything petty and annoying … In this procession of clouds there is so much smiling unconcern that I have to smile along with them, just as I always go along with the rhythm of life

around me ... As long as you never forget to look around you, you
will always be 'good' without fail.

(L: 431–432)

In Breslau, she was allowed to walk in the prison yard, but the cell
doors remained locked, so whenever she wished to walk in the yard,
she had to call a prison guard. Food rations were also very meagre
and Luxemburg's health was suffering from her protracted stay in
prison. Moreover, in autumn of that year, she received news that
Diefenbach had been killed in action. Mathilde Jacob – a loyal friend
who had put herself at grave personal risk and acted as a clandestine
courier for Luxemburg during her extended period in Barnimstrasse,
Wronke and now Breslau prisons – organised for a local family to
supply Luxemburg with extra food and other necessities (see Jacob
2000: 51–71). Luxemburg was allowed books and writing material,
and while in Breslau managed to draft the bulk of *The Russian
Revolution*, her critical analysis of the Bolshevik revolution of 1917
that, although unfinished on her release from prison, was published
posthumously in 1922 (see R: 281–310).

Luxemburg, writing from prison and at the outset of the
Bolshevik revolution, was not in a position to engage fully with the
consequences of the revolution. It is, however, important to note
some of the immediate consequences. There were appalling atrocities
on both sides as revolution toppled over into what we now think of
as Eastern Europe. Lenin's eventual triumph came at immense cost
to the region as a whole but also to his own country. The Russian
death toll from the First World War had stood at well over one and
a half million, but the revolution and the ensuing civil war added
another 3 million, while the great famine of 1921–1922 killed a
further 2 million through starvation. Across the wider region that
the Bolshevik revolution directly affected the consequences were ever
more catastrophic. As Robert Gerwarth writes,

Overall, as a result of civil war, expulsions, immigration and famine,
the population in the territories that formally became the Soviet
Union in 1922 had declined by a total of some ten million people,
from about 142 million in 1917 to 132 million in 1922.

(Gerwarth 2017: 93; see, also, Stephenson 2009: 83–90)

The Russian Revolution does not – and could not – grapple with
the moral and political consequences of the Bolshevik revolution and
its aftermath. But it does spell out with great clarity some of the
major themes that Luxemburg had been struggling with throughout
her life. She insists that, far from being achieved through adherence
to party dogma of whatever political persuasion, '[f]reedom is always
and exclusively freedom for the one who thinks differently' – and,
since thinking differently necessitates deliberation and dissent, 'the
practical realisation of socialism' can never be confined within 'a sum
of ready-made prescriptions'. 'What we possess in our program,' she
maintains, 'is nothing but a few main signposts which indicate the
general direction in which to look for the necessary measures' (R:
305).

In the final section of her analysis of the Bolshevik revolution of
1917, she accuses Lenin and Trotsky, on the one hand, and Kautsky,
on the other, of not only denying but also of repressing democracy.
Lenin and Trotsky, she argues 'decide in favour of dictatorship
in contradistinction to democracy, and thereby, in favour of the
dictatorship of a handful of persons', while Kautsky decides in favour
of 'bourgeois democracy'. Both, she insists, are failing to think outside
'the bourgeois model' whereby 'a handful of persons' – the party
vanguard in the case of Lenin and Trotsky, the educated middle class
in the case of Kautsky – is deemed to be best placed to represent the
interests of the working class. Notwithstanding their very different
political positions and perspectives, both were united in their refusal
to engage and support 'the most active, unlimited participation of the
mass of the people, of unlimited democracy' (R: 307–308).

Luxemburg was informed at 10pm on 8 November that she was
free to leave prison. Following her release, she made her way to the
office of the transport workers' union in Breslau. Given that all trains
had been suspended, she decided to remain in Breslau and address
a mass rally and demonstration due to take place the following
day. She therefore wrote a brief note to Paul Löbe, the leader of
the Breslau SPD, summoning him to meet with her in preparation
for the demonstration: 'I am at the transport workers office at 25
Rossplatz ... It is **absolutely** necessary that we come to an agreement
before the demonstration' (L: 477, emphasis in original). Her health

had deteriorated during her four years in prison. Her hair had turned grey. But the day after her release, she addressed the crowds in the central square.

The following day – 10 November – she made her way to Berlin.

THE STRUGGLE *FOR* SOCIALISM

The city was in turmoil. Across Germany an estimated 1,690,000 soldiers had died in the war. They had left behind 371,800 widows and 113,600 mothers, who had lost their sons, as well as 1,031,400 fatherless children. In addition, 2,700,000 men had been made disabled (Hagemann 2002: 12). Berlin had become a melting pot of personal sorrow and public outrage, of loss and anger, of hopelessness and resentment. The government's acknowledgement of the need for an armistice – acknowledged at the end of September – had a shattering effect on the population. But the procrastination and delay that led to the conclusion of the armistice on 11 November – with Emperor William II dithering prior to finally acknowledging that his own position was untenable and US President Wilson suspecting that Germany might be hoping to use the armistice as a preparation for renewed military action – undoubtedly heightened that effect. Two events in particular proved crucial: the naval revolt that began in Kiel and the uprising that began in Munich.

Following an order to steam out from Kiel on a suicidal attack on the British navy, the enlisted sailors rebelled. An attempt to appease the sailors by legitimising a sailor's council backfired, when, between 5 and 7 November, the sailors marched on Germany's largest naval base at Wilhelmshaven, the city hall in Hamburg, police headquarters in Braunschweig, and army garrisons in Hanover and Cologne. 'By the end of the first week of November,' as Gordon A. Craig puts it, 'the government could no longer rely on the garrisons in any of its northern cities' (1981: 400). However, it was not only in the northern cities that the government was under severe pressure. In Munich, the military headquarters were taken over on 7 November by soldiers, workers and representatives of the Bavarian Peasants' League under the leadership of Kurt Eisner, who had spent most of 1918 in prison on account of his anti-war agitation. Eisner announced the establishment of a Bavarian Republic and on 8 November established a governing cabinet.

These rapidly unfolding events led somewhat circuitously to the founding of the Weimar Republic. On the morning of 9 November, Friedrich Ebert, chair of the Reichstag group of SPD deputies, was named Reich Chancellor, thereby becoming chancellor of the German Empire over an SPD and Independent Social Democratic Party of Germany (USPD) coalition (The USPD, which was opposed to the war but ambivalent on the question of revolutionary action, had split from the SPD in 1917). At 2pm on the same day, Philipp Scheidemann, a right-wing member of the SPD and the second ranking member of the government, hearing that Liebknecht intended to declare Germany a republic sought to pre-empt him by concluding an impromptu speech to demonstrators with the words: 'The Hohenzollerns have abdicated. Long live the great German Republic!' (Craig 1981: 402). Ebert, who was no republican, was furious, but by that time, the cat was out of the bag. Late that same evening, Wilhelm II, German Emperor and King of Prussia, fled across the border into Holland. What had started as a naval rebellion had, in the space of a few days, ended in regime change. As the German historian and journalist Sebastian Haffner writes, 'what swept across Germany west of the Elbe between November 4 and 10 was a true revolution; that is to say the overthrow of the old regime and its replacement by a new one' (1973: 59).

But the new regime was itself far from revolutionary in its political intent. Within a matter of weeks, it was proving to be not only counter-revolutionary in its imposition of state control but also repressive in the means by which it sought to exert that control. Although Luxemburg refused initially to break with the SPD, she saw its leadership for what it was: anti-socialist, anti-democratic and with neither a mandate nor a vision for radical change. It had throughout the war supported global capitalism and was now opposing those who – in the appalling aftermath of defeat – were demanding an alternative future: a future which, given the social and economic crisis through which they were living, was unimaginable but *necessary*. They may not have known what that alternative future may look like or how it may feel to be part of it but they knew that without an alternative, future life would be unendurable.

Luxemburg understood that this revolutionary groundswell needed to be channelled and given a sense of direction and purpose, if it was to fulfil its potential rather than swill back into disorganised and uncoordinated protest. She used the organisational structure of the Spartacus League (formed from the International Group established in 1916) to set about this task, and on the first day of her release from Breslau, established with Karl Liebknecht the newspaper, *Die Rote Fahne* ('*The Red Flag*'), which became the main means by which she sought to provide a sense of political focus and purpose. At the same time, she was acutely aware of the effect of the political crisis on ordinary lives and families. Ten days after her release, she wrote to Marie and Adolf Geck, whose son had been killed just as the war ended:

> This is something I cannot comprehend, and tears interfere with my writing. What you are going through – I know it, I feel it, we all know the weight of this dreadful blow … I would like to help you somehow, yet there is no help, no consolation.
>
> (L: 478)

She grasped the global significance of the economic and political crisis that was unfolding across Europe, but appreciated also its crushing impact on individual lives and communities.

The Spartacus League was just one strand of what Chris Harman has described as a 'mosaic of workers' power' (1997: 52–54). Harman's metaphor is apt given the tangle of competing interests that fed into the November uprisings, although the term 'mosaic' suggests an overall design that fails to capture the unpredictability of the unfolding situation. Moreover, the phrase 'workers' power' underestimates the extent to which other powerful interests were in play during this period. If, as Haffner (1973: 59) claims, it was 'a true revolution', then it was a revolution that contained within it significant counter-revolutionary elements. In order to understand the complexity of the situation into which Luxemburg had stepped, we have to understand it as a dialectical process of claim and counter-claim, position and juxtaposition, viewpoint and opposing viewpoint: a process, that is, of struggle regarding the ends and purposes of revolution, its mode of operation and organisation, and what it means – and signifies – for current and future generations.

The struggle in the ranks

We also have to understand this situation within the context of a post-war settlement that showed a complete lack of concern for the regeneration of Germany as a viable democracy and imposed an impossible burden of reparations that seems to have been designed with a view to destroying its economy: the exchange rate, which had stood at 14 marks to the US dollar immediately after the First World War was falling to 77 marks to the dollar by July 1921, to 17,972 marks to the dollar by January 1923, and to an unimaginable 4,200,000,000,000 marks to the dollar by November 1923 (Craig 1981: 450). The nation was isolated within a European alliance intent upon exacting revenge and reducing the country to poverty and destitution. The people of Germany – as John Maynard Keynes made clear in his 1919 *The Economic Consequences of the Peace* – were being subjected to a deliberate programme of humiliation, impoverishment and selective starvation. That, as he put it, was 'abhorrent and detestable – abhorrent and detestable, even if it were possible, even if it enriched ourselves, even if it did not sow the decay of the whole civilized life of Europe' (Keynes, [1919] 2007, 127).

The Treaty of Versailles of June 1919 – and the negotiations that led to it – cast a long shadow over twentieth century Europe: a shadow the penumbra of which still lingers over an increasingly fractured twenty-first century Europe. But even before the formal ratification of the treaty, the uncertainty surrounding the outcome of the negotiations was fuelling civil unrest. Following the formal armistice and the subsequent surrender of the Reich Chancellorship to Ebert, the oppositional groupings included: the workers' councils (that had evolved largely as a result of the Kiel rebellion and its aftermath in the days prior to Luxemburg's release from prison), the USPD (which had split from the SPD in 1917), the Spartacists (of which Luxemburg had been a founding member since its formation in 1916), and a grouping generally referred to as the Left Radicals that was closely aligned to the Spartacists (but with a decidedly Bolshevik and therefore Leninist orientation).

Each of these groupings had different political agendas. 'The rank and file soldiers,' as Harman puts it, 'were fed up with war, hardship, military discipline, with eating miserable rations while their officers feasted in luxury' (1997: 52). They controlled the soldiers' and workers' councils that were springing up spontaneously not only in all the major German towns but also in Belgium and France as well as Russia. The extent to which their broad political aims extended beyond their occupational concerns no doubt varied across townships and regions, but they were a major force in the revolutionary surge of November 1918. Within this developing revolutionary situation, the USPD were compromised by their historic links with the now governing SPD, but nevertheless retained some influence within the emerging councils and maintained intermittent dialogue with the Spartacus League. But the overall situation was fluid in respect of overlapping affiliations and unpredictable in terms of what might happen when and on whose initiative. There was neither a centrally organising body, nor a formally agreed mode of decentralised control.

The Spartacus League was the ideological driving force behind the revolutionary surge. It comprised a tightly knit group, whose luminaries included Jogiches, Liebknecht, Luxemburg, Mehring and Clara Zetkin. 'Its core,' as Frölich wrote, 'was the old left-wing of Social Democracy, an elite well-grounded in Marxism and schooled in the tactical ideas of Rosa Luxemburg.' But the Spartacists also included – or were closely aligned to – what Frölich described as 'additional elements coming from varied social and political backgrounds who had been driven to the extreme left wing of the working-class movement as a result of their militant opposition to the war' (Frölich [1939] 2010: 279). Chief among these elements was the Left Radicals, a revolutionary group formed in 1917 and based in Bremen (and with close links to the Bolsheviks through one of its foremost figures, Karl Radek). Although the Spartacists worked in tandem with these elements and with the wider network of workers' and soldiers' councils, they operated according to their own organisational principles and had a clearly defined sense of membership – in a letter to Lenin dated 20 December 1918 Luxemburg referred to it as 'our family' (R: 486).

The Spartacus League helped maintain the momentum of the struggle and provide it with a sense of revolutionary purpose. Its main publishing outlet was *Die Rote Fahne*, which provided a platform not only for polemical opposition but also for serious debate regarding the future of a post-revolutionary society. Luxemburg constantly reminded her readers that revolution was not just a matter of freedom from oppression, but of the freedom of each and every individual to achieve her or his full potential: a freedom which could, she argued, only be achieved in a democratic socialist society. In arguing that case, she sought – almost to the last – to continue the struggle from within the SPD: the party for which she had fought tirelessly during the entirety of her adult life. However, the decision by Ebert, as Reich Chancellor, to ally himself with the Supreme Army Command, and thereby position the party not only as a counter-revolutionary but also as a deeply oppressive force, made a break with the SPD almost inevitable.

The formal break came in December 1918 when the Spartacus League, together with the Left Radicals, agreed to form the Communist Party of Germany (KPD). With the formation of the KPD, the 'great schism' as Schorske (1955) termed it, became a reality. Since its inception in 1875, the SPD had managed to contain its deep ideological differences on matters such as revisionism, mass action and nationalism. But in December 1918, these differences combined to create a perfect storm: the demands of radical mass action met the forces of state oppression head-on in a context fraught with nationalist sentiment and a deep resentment at the punitive and humiliating measures being demanded in the peace settlement.

Nor were these divisions fully resolved within the newly formed KPD, where one of the first questions to be addressed was whether it should take part in the elections for the National Assembly, which was to have responsibility for drawing up and ratifying the constitution of what we now refer to as the Weimar Republic. Luxemburg was in favour of participation. In an article published in the 23 December issue of *Rote Fahne*, she argued that although 'the National Assembly is a counter-revolutionary fortress erected *against* the revolutionary proletariat,' the revolutionary task is 'to expose step by step to the masses, and to appeal to the masses to intervene and force a decision.' This task, she maintained, required 'participation in the National Assembly' (quoted in Frölich [1939] 2010: 281). Luxemburg was supported within the KPD by the members of the Spartacus League, but on 30 December – at the founding conference of the KPD – she was voted down by 62 to 23.

The point at issue was implicit in that key phrase, 'step by step': a phrase, which she frequently repeated in the last months of her life. For those who opposed Luxemburg, participation in the elections was a highly questionable detour that could only delay the final victory, but for Luxemburg it was a means of ensuring that victory was viewed not as an apocalyptic finality but as a process that involved, as Frölich put it, 'careful and often very complicated manoeuvring' ([1939] 2010: 181). That process, as she pointed out in her speech to the KPD on the day following the defeat of her motion regarding participation in the National assembly elections, necessarily takes time:

> In the form that I depict it, the process may seem rather more tedious than one had imagined it at first. It is healthy, I think, that we should be perfectly clear as to all the difficulties and complications of this revolution. ... I make no attempt to prophesy how much time will be needed for this process.
>
> (R: 373)

The struggle on the streets

In that same speech, delivered on 31 December 1918, Luxemburg set out her analysis of the political situation (R: 357–373). She argued that the period between the Kiel mutiny in early November and the foundation of the KPD had constituted what she termed 'the first act' of the revolution. The major achievement of this 'first act' had been the formation of soldiers' and workers' councils that had been at the forefront of the struggle. But, she insisted, there had been a failure to confront a number of 'illusions', as a result of which this early phase of the revolution had been 'characterised by inadequacy and weakness' (R: 365). It had, for example, been based on the 'illusion' that unity and common purpose prevailed 'under the banner of so-called socialism', when in fact it had been driven as much by counter-revolutionary as by revolutionary forces. Similarly, it had all too readily accepted the 'illusion' that a 'so-called socialist government' under the leadership of Ebert and Scheidemann would bring power to the people, when its deeply repressive response to the revolution provided ample evidence that any such government would in fact 'bridle the proletarian masses' (R: 367–368).

Underlying her analysis was her long-held belief that it is impossible 'to inaugurate socialism by decree'. The events of the past four weeks had, she argued, provided ample evidence that '[s]ocialism will not and cannot be created by decrees; nor can it be established by any government, however socialistic. Socialism must be created by the masses' (R: 368). The events to which Luxemburg alluded related to two highly repressive acts undertaken by forces controlled by the Ebert–Scheidemann government: on 6 December, government forces had occupied the editorial offices of *Die Rote Fahne* – on the grounds that the Spartacus League were planning a coup – and in the ensuing demonstrations and protests had killed a number of Spartacists; on 24 December, forces had opened fire on a division of revolutionary-minded sailors in Berlin, 12 of whom, in the course of a messy and protracted stand-off, were killed. A 'so-called socialist government' had, in other words, not only sought to 'bridle the proletarian masses', but had used state violence in order to do so.

Between these two symbolic events, the government mounted a sustained propaganda war on the Spartacists in particular. 'Spartakist putsches', recalls Frölich 'were announced everyday ... Every crime was put down to the account of *Spartakus*' ([1939] 2010: 272, original emphasis and spelling). Luxemburg, along with Liebknecht and other leading Spartacists, were singled out as particular targets of vilification. The government also made every effort to influence, infiltrate and control the extensive network of soldiers' and workers' councils. As a result of these efforts, the Spartacus League was hugely under-represented at the first national congress of councils held in Berlin between 16 and 20 December: of the 489 delegates present, only ten were Spartacists. According to Haffner, the proceedings reminded journalist eyewitnesses of pre-war SPD party congresses:

'the same types, often the same faces even, the same atmosphere, conducted under the same direction, with the same concern for order and respectability ... The majority loyally supported the party executive' (1973: 113).

But the major counter-revolutionary move was to bolster the mercenary forces known as the *Freikorps* by recruiting to their ranks a number of highly trained troops, who had been demobilised under the terms of the peace agreement and who were all too ready to enlist in the highly paid mercenary force. (The first so-called *Freikorps*, or 'Free Corps', had been formed in the eighteenth century from volunteers, enemy deserters and criminals.) As the following 'call to arms' makes clear, the recruitment campaign played on the nationalist sympathies of potential recruits by raising the twin spectres of the enemy within and the enemy without:

> In the east the Russian Bolsheviks, the Poles, and the Czechs are standing on Germany's frontiers and threatening them. Inside the Reich, chaos is mounting. Plunder and disorder are everywhere. Nowhere can one find respect for law and justice, respect for personal and government property ... Therefore, we must intervene!
>
> (quoted in Craig 1981: 408)

In the weeks and months following the foundation of the KPD, the government was to rely increasingly on the *Freikorps*, under the overall command of Noske as minister of war, to spearhead the counter-revolution and crush the Spartacus League.

The events of early January 1919 showed how far the Ebert–Scheidemann government was willing to go in its attempt to regain control. These events were also crucial in the transition from, as Luxemburg put it, 'the first act of the German revolution' and 'the opening of the second act' (R: 365). Public demonstrations and protests that had erupted on Monday 5 January, together with the occupation of public buildings, met with fierce resistance. But it was from Thursday 9 January to Sunday 12 January that the government unleashed its full arsenal of state violence on the Spartacus League and the disparate and largely disorganised revolutionary groupings with which it was affiliated. As Haffner wrote,

> During this period, the Revolution in the capital was mown down with gunfire. Day after day Berliners heard the roar of cannon, previously heard only on December 24. A motley assembly of troops ... fought violent street and house-to-house battles to retake the occupied buildings one by one.
>
> (Haffner 1973: 135)

By 12 January, the fighting in Berlin was over – and, with it, what Luxemburg, in her last piece for *Die Rote Fahne*, termed 'Spartacus Week' (R: 377).

The Spartacus League was only indirectly involved in the instigation of these events, which had been triggered by a Revolutionary Committee comprising representatives from a variety of radical groupings including the KPD, the USPD and radical trade unionists. Liebknecht represented the KPD on the committee, but, given that he was a founding and leading member of the Spartacus League, had the additional responsibility of representing its views and policies. According to Frölich, Liebknecht failed to consult with either the KPD or the Spartacus League leadership and acted unilaterally in voting for action. By the time Luxemburg learned of the decision, it was too late to reverse it: '[she] quarrelled very violently with Liebknecht about his arbitrary action. Amazed and reproachful, she is reported to have said (according to Liebknecht himself) "Karl, is this our programme?"' (Frölich [1939] 2010: 289–290).

Clearly, Luxemburg felt that the action was untimely, that the groundwork had not been sufficiently prepared and that Liebknecht had failed to take into account one of the major premises of the speech she had delivered on behalf of the Spartacus League at the founding conference of the KPD, namely, the need to proceed 'step by step', with forethought and circumspection, and with a view to long-term ends and purposes. She, together with the KPD and the Spartacus League, was being drawn into revolutionary action that she considered to be ill judged, badly timed and devoid of clearly defined and agreed strategic objectives. Nevertheless, as she wrote in one of her final letters, dated 11 January and addressed to her great friend Clara Zetkin, 'one must take history as it comes, whatever course it takes' (R: 492).

We do not have Zetkin's response to Luxemburg's letter, but three years later, Zetkin wrote of the very difficult situation that the KPD had now found itself in: 'Its role in the fighting had to be at once negative and critical on the one hand, and positive and encouraging on the other' (quoted in Frölich [1939] 2010: 291). Luxemburg's own role was not only that of a major protagonist within the unfolding drama, but of someone uniquely positioned to critically comment upon it from the inside. In what she saw as its 'second act', she was both activist and interpreter. As she said in her address to the founding conference of the KPD,

[I]t is our common duty to submit to self-criticism. We shall be guided more wisely in the future, and we shall gain additional impetus for further advance, if we examine critically all that we have done and created, and all that we have left undone.

(R: 365)

The struggle for meaning

From the outset, Luxemburg was clear that the events following the naval revolt in Kiel and the uprising in Munich during the first week of November constituted the beginnings of a revolution. 'The revolution has begun,' she proclaimed in the pages of the 18 November issue of Die Rote Fahne (R: 343). But the events that comprised this revolution meant very different things to the various – and variously motivated – groups involved. For those without any clear political motivation, the events were a gesture of indignation occasioned by the humiliation of defeat and the increasingly grave economic situation; for those who were politically motivated and still maintained some residual loyalty to the 'so-called socialist government', they were an attempt to shock it into a more radical frame of mind; but for those of a politically radical persuasion who had lost all faith in the Ebert–Scheidemann government, the events were a prelude to a complete regime change.

Luxemburg was undoubtedly closest to those of a politically radical persuasion who were looking to the revolution for regime change, but with one big proviso. She not only wanted regime change, but also wanted an entirely different kind of regime: a radically new kind of decentralised, community-led and internationally oriented governance. Her experience of the 1905 Russian Revolution had confirmed her belief that organisation, although crucial, does not precede action but is the product of it. Organisation crystallises around the unfolding, unpredictable and potentially boundless consequences of action. 'The element of spontaneity,' as she wrote in her 1906 *The Mass Strike*, 'plays a great part in all Russian mass strikes without exception' – *not*, she insisted, because the Russian proletariat are 'uneducated' and prone to act before they think, 'but because revolutions do not allow anyone to play the schoolmaster with them' (R: 198). This is precisely the point on which she had already clashed with Lenin whose 'ultra-centralism', as she put it in her 1904 *Organizational Questions of Russian Social Democracy* essay, was imbued with 'the sterile spirit of the night-watchman state' (R: 256). For Luxemburg, revolution was about finding ways of broadening and strengthening the political power base, while drawing it together into radically new and outwardly looking networks of solidarity.

The 1905 revolution had also exposed the inherent conservatism of the SPD. Following electoral setbacks in January 1905, the leadership of the party was increasingly concerned with regaining seats in the Reichstag and increasingly nervous of supporting any policies that might be seen to be against the national – and indeed nationalist – interest. On her return from Poland – where she had witnessed the uprising by the Polish workers in Łódź against the Russian Empire, been imprisoned and participated in a six-day hunger strike – she became increasingly disillusioned with the SPD. Hannah Arendt, whose second husband, Heinrich Blücher, had been a member of the Spartacus League and a founding member of the KPD, wrote: 'she tried to discuss the events with her friends in the German Party … The German Socialists were convinced that such things could happen only in distant barbarian lands' (1970: 52). The support of the SPD in granting financial, and therefore moral and political, support for the First World War deepened that disillusionment into near despair – and, as Arendt points out, 'brought her near to suicide'.

So, from Luxemburg's point of view, the revolution could never be a way of pushing the SPD towards a more radical position (since the SPD had sacrificed any claim it might have to be a genuinely socialist government). Nor could it be a way of replacing one ruling regime with another (since all ruling regimes, regardless of how socialist they may claim to be, 'bridle the proletarian masses'). The only *political* justification for revolution, as far as Luxemburg was concerned, lay in the possibility of bringing about a radical shift in the power base of society such that power lies in collective action. Such action is 'spontaneous' in the sense that no individual or group assumes – or is granted – the role of 'schoolmaster' or 'nightwatchman'. It carries within it the potential for new forms of inclusive governance: forms that, as she put it in her 1918 *The Russian Revolution*, are based on 'the most active, unlimited participation of the mass of the people, of unlimited democracy' (R: 308).

From Luxemburg's perspective, the workers' and soldiers' councils were a manifestation of this urge towards 'active, unlimited participation'. They could never simply be a means to an end: a mechanism to be superseded by the party apparatchiks once the revolution had succeeded. For Luxemburg, they were embryonic of a new mode of governance. As she declared in her address to the founding conference of the KPD,

On the basis of the existing situation, we can predict with certainty that in whatever country, after Germany, the proletarian revolution may next break out, the first step will be the formation of workers' and soldiers' councils ... Precisely here lies the bond that unites our movement internationally. This is the slogan which completely distinguishes our revolution from all earlier bourgeois revolutions ... [O]n November 9 the first cry of the revolution, as instinctive as the cry of a new-born child, found the watchword which would lead us to social-ism: workers' and soldier's councils.

(R: 366)

Arendt considered Luxemburg's insight into the transformative value of collective action exercised through the workers' and soldiers' councils to be her most important legacy. The failure to grasp the significance of that insight, argued Arendt, led to the petrifaction of the Russian Revolution and its tragic transmutation into totalitarianism:

> It was nothing more or less than this hope for a transformation of the state, for a new form of government that would permit every member of the modern egalitarian society to become a 'participator' in public affairs, that was buried in the disasters of twentieth-century revolutions.
>
> (Arendt [1963] 2006: 256–257)

In struggling to elucidate the meaning of the revolutionary events in which she was participating – even when she was in the thick of those events and in grave danger – Luxemburg was attempting to imbue them with a sense of shared political purpose. The workers' and soldiers' councils brought together disparate groups that crossed party political lines and occupational divides. No party or person had ordered those groups to come together or provided them with a ready-made formula. Their power, as Luxemburg pointed out with such clear-sightedness, lay entirely in their collective self-determination. If the workers' and soldiers' councils were to be more than temporary organs of revolution, they would need not only to maintain that collective self-determination but to develop and strengthen it. That, argues Luxemburg, could only be achieved through an increased awareness of the political implications of the actions in which they were involved. One of the prime tasks she set herself, therefore, was to understand the revolution *from the inside* and to communicate that understanding – through her speeches, her writing and her letters – to all those involved in the struggle.

THE LAST DAYS

'Spartacus Week' (5–12 November) was followed by a fierce crackdown by the Ebert–Scheidemann government on individual members of the KPD and the Spartacists in particular. Luxemburg's own home was no longer a safe refuge, so she moved to the house of a friend, a doctor, in Hallesches Tor. But on 11 January, it became clear that this place was no longer safe, so she then moved in with a family in the outlying working-class area of Neukölln. On the same day, she wrote to Clara Zetkin describing the conditions that she and others were living in:

> It is impossible the way of life that I – and all of us – have been living for weeks, the tumult and turmoil, the constant changing of living quarters, the never-ending reports filled with alarm, and in between, the tense strain of work, conferences, etc., etc.
>
> (R: 490)

On Monday 13 January, she moved again to Wilmersdorf, a middle-class suburb in the south-west of Berlin, which was considered safer and where friends gave her shelter. In spite of the extreme vulnerability of her position, she refused to remain in hiding and continued to hold meetings in public and semi-public places. She may have been on the run, but she remained a public presence.

Events were taking an immense mental and physical toll on Luxemburg. In retrospect, her perseverance and resilience can be seen as heroic, but that heroism came at a tremendous cost. Frölich provides a vivid portrayal of her at this time:

> The merciless pace of the last two months, during which she expended all her energy without stint, seemed to be completing the destructive work of the war years in prison. She became subject to sudden fainting fits which happened almost every day. Advice to take rest, to place herself in the hands of a doctor, was rejected as almost treachery in the given situation, and if she noticed anyone about to broach the subject a glance was sufficient to make the words stick in his throat. A last great struggle was proceeding between her iron will and her failing body.
>
> (Frölich [1939] 2010: 293)

It was in Wilmersdorf that she produced her final piece for *Die Rote Fahne*. 'Order Reigns in Berlin' (R: 373–378) – published on 14 January – is a fiercely polemical piece that deploys all the rhetorical skills of which Luxemburg had become the supreme maestro. It is at once witheringly sarcastic, historically informed, trenchant in its analysis, and beautifully balanced as it moves from initial attack, through the modulated and more reflective central section, towards its final peroration. It is written as if it were being spoken both to a great crowd and to each and every unique individual within that crowd. It is a masterclass in political rhetoric.

The title of her piece, and the recurring rhetorical theme throughout, is a reference to the crushing by the Russian army of the Polish insurrection of 1830–1831. Following the massacre of thousands of Polish freedom fighters, the Paris Chamber of Deputies was reassured that 'Order Reigns in Warsaw': "'Order reigns in Warsaw,'" Minister Sebastiani informed the Paris Chamber of Deputies in 1831, when, after fearfully storming the suburb Praga, Paskiewitsch's rabble troops had marched into the Polish capital and begun their hangman's work on the rebels' (R: 373). General Paskiewitsch went on to crush similar uprisings in Hungary, thereby bringing to an end the revolutions begun across Europe in 1848. By evoking these past acts of state violence, Luxemburg was not only challenging any claim the Ebert–Scheidemann government might have to a social democratic lineage, but was locating the government firmly within an international and historic frame of counter-revolutionary brutality.

Having established the authoritarian and oppressive lineage of the Ebert–Scheidemann government, she went on to locate the events of 'Spartacus Week' within a revolutionary narrative that included the Communards, members of the short-lived Paris Commune formed in the wake of France's defeat in the Franco-Prussian War. In the course of the *Semaine Sanglante* ('Bloody Week'), between Sunday 21 and Sunday 28 May 1871, an estimated 20,000 communards were executed. She deploys Swift-like irony – spiked with red-hot anger – against the perpetrators of the atrocities: 'against the badly armed and starving Parisian proletarians, against their defenceless wives and children – how the manly courage of the little sons of the bourgeoisie, of the "golden youth" and of the officers flamed up again!' (R: 374). The comparison is clear, if implicit: the counter-revolutionary forces deployed by the Ebert–Scheidemann government were 'the little sons of the bourgeoisie', the gilded recipients of unearned privilege, unmanly cowards who attacked the defenceless.

She then quite abruptly switches tack and launches into a critical evaluation of 'Spartacus Week': 'What was this recent "Spartacus Week" in Berlin? What has it brought? What does it teach us?' (R: 375). She forces her readers to face the hard fact that they have just suffered defeat:

> Was an ultimate victory of the revolutionary proletariat to be expected in this conflict, or the overthrow of the Ebert–Scheidemann [government] and establishment of a socialist dictatorship? Definitely not, if all the decisive factors in this issue are taken into careful consideration.
>
> (R: 375)

Chief among these decisive factors was 'the political immaturity of the masses of soldiers'. But, she continues, 'this immaturity of the military is itself but a symptom of the general immaturity of the German revolution.' She refuses to let her readers off the hook. They cannot blame the failure on any particular group, but must take collective responsibility for it. What was lacking was 'the direct community of action' (R: 375).

At this point in her argument, she effects another abrupt turn. She asks whether, given that a conclusive and lasting victory could not be expected, the struggle of the last week was a mistake. Her answer is 'Yes, if it were in fact a matter of a deliberate "attack" or a so-called "putsch"!' But, she argues, it was no such thing. It was in response to 'brutal provocation by the government': 'Faced with the shameless provocation of the Ebert–Scheidemann [government], the revolutionary working class was forced to take up arms' (R: 375–376). They had suffered defeat. This must be acknowledged and lessons must be learnt. But that defeat also represented a 'moral victory', since:

> it was a matter of honour for the revolution to repel the attack immediately and with all due energy, lest the counter-revolution

be encouraged to advance further, and lest the revolutionary ranks of the proletariat and the moral credit of the German revolution in the International be shaken.

(R: 375–376)

This line of argument led into Luxemburg's stirring peroration in which she argued that while '[t]he whole path of socialism, as far as revolutionary struggles are concerned, is paved with sheer defeats ... yet, this same history leads "step by step", irresistibly, to the ultimate victory!' She continues: 'we are standing on precisely those defeats, not a one of which we could do without, and each of which is a part of our strength and clarity of purpose' (R: 377). What Luxemburg is saying here is paradoxical, but also deeply political in its insistence on the need to proceed 'step by step'. Some of those steps, towards a fairer and more just society, will end in defeat. Some will end in bloody defeat. But Luxemburg's point is that these defeats must be acknowledged and endured, because they help build – brick by brick – the necessary conditions for living together. Without those conditions humanity will, with the collapse of exploitative capitalist regimes, topple into barbarity.

Luxemburg concludes her final public statement by citing Ferdinand Freiligrath, a close friend of Marx: 'The revolution will "raise itself up again clashing," and to your horror it will proclaim to the sound of trumpets: *I was, I am, I shall be*' (R: 378, emphasis in original). The 'I' could so easily be taken as a reference to Luxemburg herself, but the pronoun refers back to the subject of the sentence, namely, 'the revolution'. It is the revolution that was, and is, and will be. As always, Luxemburg is looking outward and to the future.

The day after the publication of 'Order Reigns in Berlin', at 9pm on the evening of 15 January, Luxemburg along with Liebknecht and Wilhelm Pieck (a Fellow Spartacist and co-founder of the KPD) were arrested and handed over to an elite unit of the old imperial army under the command of Captain Waldemar Pabst. They were then taken to an up-market hotel named 'The Eden Hotel'. There, under the direction of Pabst, Luxemburg and Liebknecht were interrogated. Liebknecht was then led away by Pabst and members of his staff, and, on leaving the building, was struck down by rifle-butt blows to the head by a soldier named Otto Runge and dragged into a waiting car. On the way to the supposed destination of the prison in Moabit, the car pulled up. Liebknecht was dragged out, ordered to walk and then shot dead (allegedly trying to escape). The corpse was then driven to a medical facility and delivered as that of an unknown person. Shortly afterwards, Luxemburg was also taken from Eden Hotel by a Lieutenant Vogel, who was met at the door by Runge. With two blows to the skull, Runge smashed Luxemburg's skull. She was then deposited in the waiting car. She received a further blow to the head after which Vogel shot her. The corpse was then driven to Liechtenstein Bridge and thrown into the Landwehr Canal.

The counter-revolution was now operating in terror mode. Karen Hagemann writes,

> Increasingly violence became an instrument of politics. This process began in the November Revolution of 1918 ... and the mobilization of the *Freikorps* and citizen guards (*Einwohnerwehren*). It continued with the establishment of paramilitary 'protection units' by almost the entire spectrum of political groupings and the militarization of demonstration culture, including the wearing of uniforms. It culminated in meeting-hall and street terror and political assassination.
>
> (Hagemann 2002: 15)[3]

On 25 January, 32 of those killed in 'Spartacus Week' were buried with Liebknecht. On 10 March, Jogiches was arrested and suffered the same fate as Liebknecht: shot while allegedly trying to escape. On 31 May, Luxemburg's body was discovered washed up at one of the locks of the canal, and – under Noske's orders – kept at a local army camp prior to burial. The funeral was held at Friedrichs-felde Cemetery on 13 June. A large crowd of mourners attended the service but, under the watchful eye of Noske's forces, the public demonstration of support for Luxemburg was silent and compliant. By the middle of 1919, the German Revolution had been all but broken, its leaders and many of its activists having been rounded up into concentration camps or summarily murdered.

Although a military court was set up to establish the circumstances surrounding the deaths of Liebknecht and Luxemburg, those with direct responsibility for their murder were either spirited away or received minimal sentences. The failure to acknowledge the enormity of the crime, or to bring the perpetrators to justice, ensured the final splintering of the left in Germany and the subsequent failure of any coordinated opposition to the rise of fascism within Germany in the decades that followed. Indeed, many of those central to or carrying out the orders of the 'so-called socialist government' of Ebert and Scheidemann, including those with direct responsibility for Luxemburg's murder, ended their careers as enthusiastic supporters of Adolf Hitler and the Nazi regime. In 1933, her books were publically burned and the cemetery where she had been buried was subsequently razed to the ground by the Nazis. Under Stalin, her legacy was similarly erased and traduced. 'Many of her comrades-in-arms and pupils, both German and Polish,' as Frölich recorded, 'paid for their faithfulness to her ideas in Stalin's prison-camps, and many were shot to death after having been robbed of their revolutionary honour' ([1939] 2010: 302).

Across Europe, the post-First World War period was one of immense political turmoil and extreme violence, with civil wars, nationalist wars and revolutions being the norm rather than the exception across the region. Between 1917 and 1920, Europe experienced 27 violent transfers of political power, many of them accompanied by civil wars. As Gerwarth has argued:

Not since the Thirty Years' War of the seventeenth century had a series of interconnected wars and civil wars in Europe been as inchoate and deadly as in the years after 1917–18. As civil wars overlapped with revolutions, counter revolutions and border conflicts between emerging states without clearly defined frontiers or internationally recognized governments, 'post-war' Europe between the official end of the Great War in 1918 and the Treaty of Lausanne in July 1923 was the most violent place on the planet.
(Gerwarth 2017: 7)

Even excluding the millions who perished as a result of the Spanish flu pandemic between 1918 and 1920 – or the hundreds of thousands who starved to death as a consequence of the economic blockade imposed by the victors of the war after the cessation of hostilities – well over 4 million died as a result of armed conflict in post-First World War Europe (Hawkins 2002; Osborne 2004; Phillips and Killingray 2003; Vincent 1985).

In the light of this appalling tragedy, with its backdrop of bloodshed and inhumanity, it is all too easy to view Luxemburg as a tragic victim of fate, whose life was violently cut short at the beginning of a doomed revolution over which she exercised very little influence and even less control. Haffner, for example, claims that:

> Everything would have happened exactly as it did if [Liebknecht and Rosa Luxemburg] had not existed … In those days from November 9 to January 15, in what remained of their lives, [they] worked like people possessed, to the very limits of their strength: but they effected nothing.
>
> (Haffner 1973: 143)

But to define Luxemburg solely in terms of the two months preceding her brutal death is to run the risk of reducing her complex and multifarious life to a caricature: a heroic caricature perhaps, but a caricature nonetheless. To understand the full 'effect' of her life's work and its significance for us in the twenty-first century, we need to consider it in a broader context and with reference to a more extensive time-span.

Taking the long view, history can be seen to support Luxemburg's claim that the revolution would raise itself up again and proclaim '*I was, I am, I shall be*'. As Arendt pointed out, there is a clear line of continuity that can be traced from the soldiers' and workers' councils of the German Revolution through to the councils that played such a crucial role in the Hungarian Revolution of 1956:

> councils of writers and artists, born in the coffee houses of Budapest, student's and youths' councils at the universities, workers councils in the factories, councils in the army, among the civil servants …

The formation of a council in each of these disparate groups turned
a more or less accidental proximity into a political institution.
(Arendt [1963] 2006: 258–259)

Moreover, that line of continuity can be traced from the Hungarian
Revolution through the Prague Spring of 1968, the Revolutions of
1989 and the 'Arab Spring' of 2011, to what Immanuel Ness (2016)
has termed the 'Southern Insurgency' of workers in China, India and
South Africa.

Like the German Revolution of 1918–1919, these acts of collective
protest and creative defiance can be seen as part of a much longer and
still ongoing struggle for democratic socialism. Luxemburg grasped
with amazing clear-sightedness what Raymond Williams called the
'extremely damaging' consequences of '[t]he conventional opposition
between democracy and socialism' (1979a: 426). She also intuited that
this opposition was to be one of the major ideological battlegrounds
of the twentieth and twentieth-first centuries. Her enduring
legacy comprises the resources – ideas and insights, arguments and
analyses, questions and challenges – that she gathered to ensure that
democratic socialism would eventually win not only against what
she called 'bourgeois democracy' but also against any form of non-
socialist democracy or non-democratic socialism.

* * *

The following three chapters shift from biographical narrative to a
broader discussion of Luxemburg's ideas. She was, as we have seen,
a writer and thinker of immense range and talent. She was at once
a hard-headed polemicist, a formidable economic theorist, a highly
original political thinker and one of the great letter writers of the
early twentieth century. Across her numerous writings, a number of
key themes emerge, never quite evolving into a political theory but
providing a coherent structure of ideas. These themes focus on the
nature of political struggle, political agency and political purpose.
Running through these themes is a continuing emphasis on the
potential of critical consciousness to generate new social, critical and
future imaginaries.

PART II

The World Upside Down

*Socialists are not in the least thinking of turning the world upside down,
for it is upside down already.*

Rosa Luxemburg, 1900, 'In Defence of Nationality' (RPL: 42)

3

Political Struggle

Luxemburg never ceased from what William Blake called 'mental fight'. Her politics were enacted on the street and in the head, on the campaign trail and at the desk, on the political platform and in her private letters to friends and associates. Her activism was inseparable from her thinking. She wrote with passion and precision on economics and the history of capitalism, the social conditions of the working class, and the theory and practice of political action. She spoke with an acute sense of occasion, audience and purpose. She was undoubtedly one of the greatest political orators of her generation, whose ideas were constantly shaping her political outlook. Her seeming spontaneity of judgement was always the result of the long struggle to relate ideas to words, to get the words in the right order, and to get the timing right. She was not a 'public intellectual' in the sense that we now use that term, but she put her intellect unconditionally at the disposal of what she saw as the common good. She was a public educator, an activist, a revolutionary and a supremely important political thinker.

Her ideas and political outlook developed and matured over time, in response to changing circumstances, personal relationships, and – always – her critical analysis of current events. It took years for her to arrive at a fully articulated position regarding the economics of capital accumulation, as elaborated in her 1913 *The Accumulation of Capital*, and a further two years to respond fully, in the form of her *Anti-Critique* drafted in Barnimstrasse Women's Prison in Berlin between 1915 and 1916, the 'epigones', whose critiques of her work were in her view based on an uncritical imitation of Marx (see CW II: 1–342, 343–449). Throughout this same period, she was participating in and drawing crucial insights from the mass actions periodically erupting across Europe and notably within Russia – as evidenced in her 1904 essay on *Organisational Questions of Russian Social Democracy*, her 1906 *Mass Strike* pamphlet, and her *The Russian Revolution* pamphlet of 1918 (see R: 248–265, 168–199, 281–310). She was continually learning from fellow activists, in particular the workers with whom she electioneered and demonstrated and those enrolled at the SPD School in Berlin. Throughout her life, she was struggling to bring the economic, political and social strands of her thinking into a coherent whole.

Her intellectual and political formation took place within the context of the Second International (1889–1916). Here the struggle over revisionism within the SPD, the use of mass action and the response to nationalism dominated the political debate. Although she found an increasingly dysfunctional home within the SPD, she was always a child of an equally fractious and sectarian Second International. But the Second International did at least provide a forum for radical debate and held out some hope of an international coalition committed to democratic socialism. Its collapse at the outset of the First World War – coupled with what she saw as the betrayal by the SPD leadership – led to her near despair. Nevertheless, it was within this broader context of internationalised political debate that she mounted a radical critique of the centralising tendencies manifest in 'bourgeois democracy' and emergent in Bolshevik socialism. In so doing, she highlighted both the necessity for democratic renewal in the struggle for socialism and the necessary commitment to socialism in any struggle for democratic renewal. The two were inextricably entwined. 'Socialism', as Frölich put it in characterising Luxemburg's world-view, 'is democracy completed, the free unfolding of the individual personality through working together with all for the well-being of all' (Frölich [1939] 2010: xx).

But it is only within a broader contextual frame of time and place that we can understand the full effect of her life's work. Viewed from the perspective of the twenty-first century, what – if anything – is Luxemburg's lasting significance? She undoubtedly remains an iconic figure for those still grieving the passing of a bygone age of collective socialism: the 'Red Rosa' of socialist legend. But she also remains a hugely important presence for those who are committed to rethinking the idea of socialism within a world of difference and deep uncertainty. Luxemburg believed passionately that Marxism could speak to the new and changing conditions of the early twentieth century. But she also realised that, in order to do so, the Marxist legacy would need to be re-interpreted, re-thought and re-activated. Some of its central tenets would need to be questioned, or even jettisoned, while others would need to be refined and developed. Her true legacy lies in this capacity for critical re-interpretation.

Three areas of critical re-interpretation, as advanced by Luxemburg, are of continuing relevance within the debate on the future of democratic socialism. These constitute the major themes in Luxemburg's political thought and provide the central thematic of this and the following two chapters.

First, she understood that the political sphere could no longer be defined exclusively, or even primarily, in economic terms. The Marxist tradition she inherited had focused on economic freedom. Luxemburg broadened the argument by showing that the struggle for socialism cannot be limited to the economic sphere. It was, in other words, not just a struggle for economic freedom but for social and civic freedom. As such, it relied on solidarities that are based not only on economic exploitation but also on social exploitation and exclusion, and on political disenfranchisement. Notwithstanding her academic background in economic theory, Luxemburg took from the tradition she inherited an insight into the economy as embedded within a social and civic nexus. Her work provides a bridge from a notion of 'the political' as predominantly economic to one in which the economic, the social and the civic are inextricably enmeshed: 'the political' as a confirmation of what Sheldon S. Wolin has called 'the idea that a free society composed of diversities can nonetheless enjoy moments of commonality when, through public deliberations, collective power is used to promote or protect the well-being of the collectivity' (Wolin 2016: 100).

Second, she emphasised the central importance of critical con-sciousness in the formation of any oppositional movement. She questioned the traditional assumption that such a movement already existed fully formed within society. While wholeheartedly committed to the working class as an indispensable element in any oppositional movement, she saw the proletariat not as an already existing revolutionary subject but as a revolutionary subject in the making. As the industrial working class has become a decreasing minority among wage-workers, Luxemburg's emphasis on consciousness as a major component in the formation of oppositional groups has become increasingly relevant. Opposition is formed on the basis of a commonality of critical perspective; it does not come ready-made as a function of a particular class. Luxemburg was, of course, unaware of the profound technological changes that would transform the labour market and usher in the post-industrial society. Nevertheless, her work can again be seen as a bridge between an analysis grounded in the experience of capitalist exploitation within early industrialised society and analyses that confront the exploitative mechanisms of late, post-industrial capitalism.

Third, she insisted on the indeterminacy of history. She was enough of an historical determinist to believe that capitalism would eventually implode under the weight of its own imperialist exploitation: that there would come a time when the earth's resources had finally been exhausted and capitalism would simply collapse into a human and natural void of its own making. But she continually rejected the idea that this collapse would inevitably herald the dawn of socialism. On the contrary, she believed that the collapse of socialism would result in unimaginable barbarity unless the conditions necessary for socialism had been put in place. To that extent, she rejected historical determinism in favour of a view of history as open-ended and always not-yet-finished. The future is what we make of it through deliberation and collective action, not what ideology defines it as. Here again Luxemburg can be seen as providing a bridge from what was, for her, an inherited assumption regarding the historical inevitability of human progress to a perspective that acknowledges the uncertainty and unpredictability of human history. We cannot know in advance what the new social organisations of freedom will look like. We have to think our way towards them. We have to re-imagine 'the political'.

In the final sentences of one of her last theoretical works (*An Anti-Critique*), Luxemburg highlighted what this re-imagining involved and how, in her view, it was central to the Marxist tradition within which – and against which – she developed her own thinking:

> Marxism is a revolutionary outlook on the world that must always strive toward new knowledge and new discoveries. Nothing is so abhorrent to it as to grow rigid in forms that were once appropriate but no longer are. Its living force is best preserved in the intellectual clash of self-criticism and in the midst of history's thunder and lightning.
>
> (CW II: 448–449)

For Luxemburg, Marxism was a living, changing tradition of thought and practice. It provided her not only with a conceptual apparatus, but also with a mode of practical reasoning which – as Andrea Nye (1994: 49) puts it – enabled her 'to think generally and concretely at the same time' and, in doing so, to give 'attention to concrete, day-to-day events along with attention to the most abstract of economic theories'.

THE DIALECTICS OF STRUGGLE

Luxemburg viewed economic exploitation, the social conditions resulting from that exploitation and collective acts of resistance as constituting core elements within a single process of political struggle. She saw this process – and the elements that comprise it – not as a linear progression from one discrete phase to the next, but as one of crystallisation: resistance coalescing around a collective awareness of how capitalism impacts on social well-being, and, crucially, of how society speaks back to capitalist exploitation through new and emergent social formations. History, from this perspective, is not predetermined. Nor is it entirely indeterminate. It is determined by how – at precise points and within specific sectors – we choose to act.

Her central insight, developed in the *Introduction to Political Economy* (her unfinished book begun in around 1908 and based on her lectures to the SPD School in Berlin between 1907 and 1914) and elaborated in her 1913 *The Accumulation of Capital*, is that capitalism is at once dependent upon and at the same time deeply exploitative of pre-capitalist societies. In the former work, she shows the extent of that exploitation through a detailed analysis of the dissolution of ancient Germanic, Greek, Indian, Russian and South American forms of village organisation based on common ownership. She does not attempt to sentimentalise or romanticise these primitive forms of communal living. On the contrary, she shows how in their various formations and transmutations, they may lead to tribalism, feudalism and even enslavement. 'Primitive communist society,' she insists, 'through its own internal development leads to the formation of inequality and despotism' (CW I: 233).

But she is equally adamant that 'European civilization' destroyed whatever economic, social and political potential these primitive communist societies might have had:

> The intrusion of European civilization was a disaster in every sense for primitive social relations ... European capitalism deprives the primitive social order of its foundation. What emerges is something that is worse than all the oppression and exploitation, total anarchy and that specifically European phenomenon of the uncertainty of social existence. The subjugated peoples, separated from their means of production, are regarded by European capitalism as mere laborers; if they are useful for this end, they are made into slaves, and if they are not, they are exterminated ... [V]iolence is merely the servant of economic development.
>
> (CW I: 234)

In *The Accumulation of Capital*, Luxemburg elaborates further this link between capitalism's dependency on – and unremitting violence towards – non-capitalist forms of production. Capitalism, she argues,

> requires noncapitalist social strata as a market in which to realize its surplus value, as a source for its means of production and as a reservoir of labor-power for its wage system ... Therefore capitalism above all wages a constant war of annihilation everywhere against any historical form of natural economy that it encounters.
>
> (CW II: 265)

The crucial word here is 'constant'. Capitalism's war against non-capitalist and pre-capitalist forms of production is not a matter of
a one-off conquest, but is part of the ongoing historical process:
'Capital knows no other solution to the problem than violence, which
has been a constant method of capital accumulation as a historical
process, not merely during its emergence, but also to the present day'
(CW II: 267).

Political violence

In order to grasp the relation between capitalism and violence, the
economy has to be understood *politically*. In the first chapter of her
Introduction to Political Economy, Luxemburg sets about this task.
In that opening chapter, she poses the question, 'What is political
economy?' In the course of addressing that question, she argues
that capitalism assumes the existence of what she terms a 'world
economy' reliant on international trade, behind which lies 'a whole
network of economic entanglements, which have nothing to do with
simple commodity exchange' (CW I: 115). The 'world economy', in
other words, is not simply a 'national economy' writ large. Nor does
it correspond to a fair trade zone between equal trading partners.
On the contrary: 'The European "national economies" extend their
polyp-like tentacles to all countries and people of the earth, strangling
them in a great net of capitalist exploitation' (CW I: 116).

   She then goes on to provide a stark example of how the 'whole
network of economic entanglement' unfolds over time to create
widening circles of global exploitation and human suffering. Her
starting point was the early industrial revolution in England and the
building of the first mechanically driven cotton spinning plant in
Nottingham in the late eighteenth century. 'The immediate result
in England,' she argues, 'was the destruction of handloom weaving
and the rapid spread of mechanical manufacture' (CW I: 116). Since
the cotton industry drew its raw material from North America,
'[t]he growth of factories in Lancashire conjured up immense cotton
plantations in the southern United States' (CW I: 116), as a result of
which '[t]he African slave trade expanded tremendously ... At the
end of the eighteenth century, in 1790, there were by one estimate

only 697,000 blacks; in 1861 there were over four million' (CW I: 116–117).

This 'colossal extension' of the slave trade and slave labour in the southern states of the USA prompted a reaction in the northern states:

> The fabulous business of the Southern planters, who could drive their slaves to death within seven years, was all the more intolerable to the pious Puritans of the North because their own climate prevented them from establishing a similar paradise in their own states.
>
> (CW I: 117)

At the instigation of the northern states, the Emancipation Proclamation granted freedom to all slaves in the Confederate states on 1 January 1863, though this could only be enforced when and where these states were occupied by Union forces. The southern states thereby declared their secession from the Union, and the civil war broke out – the immediate effect of which was 'the devastation and economic ruin of the Southern states. Production and trade collapsed, the supply of cotton was interrupted' (CW I: 117).

At that point, this particular cycle of exploitation came full circle: the interruption of the supply of cotton

> deprived English industry of its raw material, and in 1863 a tremendous crisis broke out in England, the so called 'cotton famine'. In Lancashire, 250,000 workers lost their jobs completely, 166,000 were only employed part-time, and just 120,000 were still fully employed.
>
> (CW I: 117)

But, as Luxemburg shows, this cycle of exploitation was only part of a more extensive cyclical entanglement. Denied the American supply of cotton, 'English industry sought to obtain its raw materials elsewhere, and turned its attention to the East Indies.' In doing so, it supplanted traditional rice cultivation, 'which had provided the daily food of the population for millennia and formed the basis of their existence' (CW I: 117). As a consequence, 'the next few years saw an extraordinary price rise and a famine that carried off over a million people in Orissa alone, a district north of Bengal' (CW I: 118).

The capitalist world economy, insists Luxemburg, must be understood in terms of the political violence, which is intrinsic to the process of capital accumulation. Moreover, that understanding must be informed by a broad historical perspective:

> a history that winds its way through all five continents, hurls millions of lives hither and thither, erupting in one place as economic crisis, in another as famine, flaming up here as war, there as revolution, leaving in its wake on all sides mountains of gold and abysses of poverty – a wide and blood-stained stream of sweat from human labor.
>
> (CW I: 120)

The crucial point that Luxemburg insists upon – and that is fully elaborated in her *The Accumulation of Capital* – is that the political violence inflicted by capitalism is not an unfortunate side effect of the capitalist mode of production.

Rather, at both the point of production ('the factories, the mines, the farms') and at the point of intersection between capitalist and non-capitalist forms of production ('colonial policy, the system of international credit, the policy spheres of interest, and war') political violence is fundamental to capitalism's modus operandi:

> political violence is nothing but a vehicle for the economic process; both sides of capital accumulation are organically bound up with each other through the very conditions of the reproduction of capital, and it is only together that they result in the historical trajectory of capital.
>
> (CW II: 329)

Then, as now, capitalism results in social suffering in the particular social and working environments where surplus value is produced and through a global economy that maintains and protects the increasing concentration of wealth – and unaccountable power – of those who reap the rewards of that surplus value.

Social suffering

If the economy has to be understood in terms of the political violence it inflicts, then society has to be understood in terms of the social suffering that results from that violence. The capitalist world economy, argues Luxemburg in her *Introduction to Political Economy*, impacts hugely on social relations and individual identity through, for example, recurring trade crises, unemployment and fluctuating prices. These are endemic to capitalism, but operate independently of human will and intentionality. The 'puzzle' as she puts it – the disparity between intention and result – lies at the heart of the social dislocation experienced within capitalism. A trade crisis – resulting, for example, from over-production and insufficient demand – is seen and treated by all those involved:

> as something that stands outside the realm of human will and human calculation, like a blow of fate inflicted on us by an invisible power, a test from heaven of the same order as the severe storm, an earthquake or a flood.
>
> (CW I: 128)

The crisis is neither wanted nor wished for: 'No one wants the crisis, and yet it comes. People create it with their own hands, yet they do not intend it for anything in the world' (CW I: 129).

Similarly, unemployment, which, she argues, has become 'to a greater or lesser degree, a constant and everyday accompaniment to economic life', is 'not an element, a natural phenomenon of physics, but a purely human product of economic relations.' It is not simply that human beings cannot resolve the problems that are of their own making, but that they cannot identify those problems:

> once again here we come up against an economic puzzle, a phenomenon that no one intended, no one consciously strove for,

but which all the same appears with the regularity of a natural phenomenon, over people's heads as it were.

(CW I: 131)

Price fluctuations, too, fall into this category of 'puzzlement' whereby society becomes dislocated from individual will:

> Price fluctuations are likewise a secretive movement … And yet commodity prices and their movements are obviously a purely human affair, with no magic involved. It is no one but people themselves who produce commodities with their own hands and determine their prices … here again, the need, end and result of people's economic action come into blatant imbalance.

(CW I: 132)

This 'blatant imbalance' is matched by the glaring disparity between a strictly managed and regulated work place and the wholly unpredictable workings of the global market: 'if we look at an individual private firm, a modern factory or a large complex of factories and plants … we find here the strictest organization … Here everything works beautifully, directed by a *single* will and consciousness' (CW I: 134, emphasis in original). But, as she goes on to point out, 'we scarcely leave the factory or farm gate than we are met already with chaos … [W]hereas the fragments are most strictly organized, the whole of the so-called "national economy", i.e. the capitalist world economy, is completely unorganized' (CW I: 134).

Pursuing this theme later in the *Introduction to Political Economy*, in the chapter on 'commodity production', Luxemburg argues that the only regulatory authority within this unorganised global economy is that of commodity exchange: 'Exchange itself now regulates the whole economy mechanically … [I]t creates a link between the individual producers, it forces them to work, it governs their division of labour, determines their wealth and its distribution. Exchange governs society' (CW I: 241). Pre-capitalist societies based on common ownership may have been 'ossified … rather immovable and rigid', but they constituted 'a compact whole … a firm organism'. Capitalist societies, on the other hand, are characterised by unpredictability and endless flux: 'Now we have an extremely loose structure, in which the individual members keep falling away and then reassembling' (CW I: 241).

The effect of this 'extremely loose structure' on the worker, and on how the worker relates to society, is profound: 'No one bothers about him, he does not exist for society. He only informs society of his existence by the fact that he appears on the commodity market with a product of his labour' (CW I: 241). The logic of capitalism requires a restructuring of society such that commodity exchange becomes its defining feature. Other forms of human exchange – and inter-change – may continue, but these now reassemble around the overriding priority of production and consumption. The result is a new kind of society – 'an extremely loose and mobile society' – in which individuals pursue their private interests and commodity production is the condition of life:

> a state of society thereby comes into being in which people all lead their particular existence as completely separate individuals, who do not exist for each other, but only through their commodities attain a constantly fluctuating membership of the whole, or again excluded from membership.
>
> (CW I: 242)

In developing this line of argument, Luxemburg was building on Marx's arguments on commodity and exchange in the first part of Volume I of Marx's *Capital*, but she was also laying some of the foundations for the ground-breaking work undertaken by Georg Lukács. Begun in 1922, his studies in Marxist dialectics were not widely accessible until 1968, but drew heavily on Luxemburg's legacy. Under capitalism, argued Lukács, '[t]he commodity ... becomes the universal category of society as a whole' ([1968] 1971: 86). Within such a society, 'a man's activity becomes estranged from himself'. It becomes a 'thing'. The individual becomes a cog in the machine: 'Neither objectively nor in his relation to his work does man appear as the authentic master of the process; on the contrary, he is mechanical part incorporated into a mechanical system' (Lukács [1968] 1971: 89). Central to Lukács' argument is that this process whereby human

beings become alienated from their own actions and their consciousness – a process that he termed 'reification' – is not only identifiable in
the objective reality of the market economy, but informs and shapes
our subjective experience and intersubjective relations: 'Reification
is, then, the necessary, immediate reality of every person living in a
capitalist society' ([1968] 1971: 197).

Just as political violence is intrinsic to the workings of a global
capitalist economy, so the social suffering that results from that violence
cannot be seen simply – and naively – as one of its unfortunate and
unintended consequence. A capitalist mode of production whereby
surplus value is distilled into a constantly accumulating reservoir
of private wealth is premised on the assumption of an exponential
increase in inequality: an increase not only in the proportion of those
suffering the big sorrows (*la grande misère*) of absolute poverty, but
also those suffering the little sorrows (*la petite misère*) of relative
poverty and its social fall-out. This *positional suffering*, as Pierre
Bourdieu and his colleagues have termed it, can all too easily be
dismissed with responses such as 'You really don't have anything
to complain about' or 'You could be worse off, you know'. But, as
Bourdieu and his colleagues go on to argue,

> using material poverty as the sole measure of all suffering keeps us
> from *seeing* and understanding a whole side of the suffering char-
> acteristic of a social order which [has] set up the conditions for an
> unprecedented development of all kinds of ordinary suffering (*la
> petite misère*).
>
> (Bourdieu *et al.* 1999: 4)

The axis of history

In Luxemburg's thinking, the economic, the social and the political
form a recurrent dialectic: the capitalist economy inflicts political
violence on those who contribute to the accumulation of capital; that
political violence results in particular and historically located forms
of social suffering; but – and crucially – the growing consciousness of
the political violence inflicted by the capitalist mode of production
is itself a necessary condition for resistance and the re-imagining of

an alternative society. It is, maintains Luxemburg, in the particularity of our social and economic situations that we discover the resources necessary for political resistance. Prime among these resources is a shared critical consciousness of how political violence operates. The other resources – which, for Luxemburg, include friendship and comradeship, hope in the face of seeming defeat and a deep sense of international solidarity – follow from a shared understanding of how the past has shaped our present circumstances and of how we, in turn, might begin to shape our collective futures.

History does not arrive ready-made, but is always in the making. It does not simply unfold, revealing a grand pattern (as in the unfolding of a Persian carpet) or a grand narrative (as in the un-scrolling of an ancient script). It is, rather, the unpredictable concatenation of myriad actions and their consequences – forever melding and coalescing, fracturing and splintering, circling and spiralling – that constitutes human history. History, in other words, is grounded in the complex and unpredictable interplay of consequentiality. Goethe's famous quotation from Faust – 'in the beginning was the deed' (R: 255) – lay at the heart of Luxemburg's notion of history and the implicit theory of action that informs all her writing and thinking. If deeds – rather than the Word, the Logos, the Enlightenment – constitute our beginning, and if the consequences that flow from those deeds collide and coalesce unpredictably, then agency precedes organisation. Action, not organisational intent, is 'the axis of intellectual crystalli-sation' (R: 161); or, as Luxemburg put it in her 1904 *Organisational Questions of Russian Social Democracy*: 'Organization, enlightenment and struggle are here not separate moments mechanically divided in time ... they are merely different facets of the same process' (R: 252).

That same essay, in which Luxemburg takes Lenin to task for what she sees as his 'uncompromising centralism' (R: 250), concludes with a direct address to her readership within the SPD and across the international boundaries of the Second International: 'Finally, let us speak frankly between ourselves: the mistakes that are made by a truly revolutionary workers' movement are, historically speaking, immeasurably more fruitful and more valuable than the infallibility of the best possible "Central Committee"' (R: 250). The assumptions underlying this statement are crucial to Luxemburg's world-view.

She acknowledges that collective revolutionary action is subject to contingent factors and therefore susceptible to defeats and setbacks ('mistakes'). But she also insists that these defeats and setbacks have greater potential for revolutionary action ('more fruitful and more valuable') than a perfectly designed ('infallible') plan. Defeats and setbacks are not only intrinsic to the revolutionary struggle, but offer insight, opportunity and the possibility of new perspectives.

Central to Luxemburg's thinking is the distinction between the organisation and discipline associated with 'uncompromising centralism' and the decentralised forms of organisation and discipline that can – given the right historical circumstances – crystallise around action. This distinction underlies her personal relationships, her political activism, her teaching within the SPD School in Berlin and her work as a political economist. It is a distinction to which she continually returns, as when she comments (in a letter dated 2 October 1905) on a book by her friend Henriette Roland Holst-van der Schalk: 'you discuss the mass strike much too formalistically ... and in that connection you put too much emphasis on the aspect of organisation and discipline and much too little on the **historical** process'. She then goes on to elaborate on this fairly blunt critique of her friend's work: 'you haven't spelled out enough that from this context the mass strike emerges as an elementary phenomenon' (R: 191, emphasis in original).

Collective action, as exemplified in the mass strike, is a 'phenomenon' in the sense that it claims a presence – an appearance – on the streets and in the public thoroughfares; it is 'elementary' in the sense that it requires no organisational prerequisite. The only discipline required of collective action lies in the shared understanding of those involved. Lukács, in his 1921 essay on Luxemburg, singled out this insight into the relation between action and organisation as one of her major intellectual contributions to Marxism: 'Rosa Luxemburg perceived at a very early stage that the organisation is much more likely to be the effect than the cause of the revolutionary process' (Lukács [1968] 1971: 41). There is, in other words, no way to rise above – or beyond – the historical process in order to organise it *from the outside*: no ahistorical position that is above or beyond the fray. You have to act within it and to understand it *from within*.

On the basis of that understanding, organic forms of democratic participation and organisation may emerge and flourish. It was because of her belief in the efficacy of such democratic forms of resistance that – in her 1906 pamphlet on the mass strike – she inveighed against those conservative elements in the SPD and among the trade union leadership who attempted to discredit and stifle them: the 'nightwatchmen', as she called them, who adhere to and promote 'the policeman-like theory that the whole modern labor movement is an artificial, arbitrary product of a handful of conscienceless "demagogues and agitators"'. The Russian Revolution of 1905, she continues, teaches us that 'the mass strike is not artificially "made", not "decided" at random, not "propagated," but that it is an historical phenomenon which, at a given moment, results from social conditions with historical inevitability' (R: 170).

Similarly, the workers' and soldiers' councils that were formed in the wake of the November 1918 Kiel uprising were a significant instance of organically generated formations of resistance that Luxemburg interpreted as the nucleus of an emergent democratic socialism. She insisted, in one of her final articles for *Die Rote Fahne*: 'Only through constant, vital, reciprocal contact between the masses of the people and their organs, the workers' and soldiers' councils, can the activity of the people fill the state with a socialist spirit' (R: 351). Luxemburg was to the end of her life always thinking about the organisational implications of human action as they played out within the broader spectrum of history. But she was adamant that human action is the axis of history and that we can only understand history from our particular economic, social and temporal location within it. We understand the historical process not as stargazers looking through a telescope or objective analysts looking through a microscope, but as human agents who seek a perspective from within that process.

The axis of history is the here and now: the pivotal point between past and present at which we realize our human agency through action. Luxemburg reminds us, over and over again, that this realization can only occur when we act *knowingly* and *together*. Collective action has its roots in the social. So, while society is shaped by the political violence of an economic system that relies on the exploitation of human and natural resources, it speaks back to that violence through the collective power of new and emergent social formations, fragile forms of democratic participation and social movements that discover their political will and purpose through action: 'socialism', as Axel Honneth puts it, 'necessarily aims to make modern society more "social" in the full sense of the term by unleashing forces or potentials already contained in the current society' (2017: 52).

SOCIAL IMAGINARIES

Arguing for the importance of a 'full concept of determination', Raymond Williams (1977) distinguished between 'negative determinations' that are experienced as limits and 'positive determinations' that are experienced as acts of will or purpose. 'For in practice,' as he puts it, 'determination is never only the setting of limits; it is also the exertion of pressures.' 'Positive determinations' may serve to maintain and reinforce 'negative determinations', as when, for example, we opt for courses of action or ways of thinking that limit the realization of our full potential. But, maintains Williams, '[t]hey are also, and vitally, pressures exerted by new formations, with their yet unrealized intentions and demands.' In the light of this 'full concept of determination', 'society' is never only a 'dead husk', which sets limits on social and individual fulfilment: 'It is always also a constitutive process with very powerful pressures which are both expressed in political, economic and cultural formations' (1977: 87).

This complex process of 'determination' is both dialectical and indeterminate: 'dialectical' in that it involves the struggle between contrary tendencies; and 'indeterminate' in that the outcome of that struggle can only be ascertained through engaging in that struggle. We cannot know in advance whether new and emergent elements – new meanings and values, new practices, new relationships and kinds of relationship – will in practice reinforce the dominant order or exert oppositional pressure upon it, since, as Williams points out, 'it is exceptionally difficult to distinguish between those which are really elements of some new phase of the dominant culture ... and those which are substantially alternative or oppositional to it' (1977: 123). It was because of the indeterminacy of this process that Luxemburg was constantly reminding her friends and associates that they must proceed 'step by step'; that self-criticism was a vital element in ensuring that new, emergent and vital elements, such as the workers and soldiers' councils, remained true to purpose; and that the capacity to endure defeats and setbacks – and, crucially to look beyond them – were among the indispensable attributes of the political activist.

Notwithstanding her attentiveness to the ever-present possibility of 'negative determinations' – or what she would have termed counter-revolutionary elements – Luxemburg focused primarily on identifying the spaces within which 'positive determinations' might flourish: spaces of critical consciousness in which people are bound by a shared understanding of how capitalist exploitation works; spaces of collective action in which people act on that shared consciousness and thereby express their political agency; spaces of freedom in which, through that consciously driven collective action, people demand not only economic freedom – freedom from economic dependency – but the social freedom to move beyond that dependency into genuinely new forms of social engagement. These were, for Luxemburg, both local and global spaces. They included those at the point of production – the workers who produced the surplus value upon which capitalism relied – and those at the receiving end of imperialist expansion and colonial subjugation.

They were, of course, imagined spaces. But Luxemburg dared to imagine them. Moreover, she imagined them not as some distant utopia, but as a realisable and concrete reality. In her December 1918 'The Socialization of Society' – one of her last pieces written on the run and while in extreme danger of capture and execution – she provided one of her fullest discussions of what she saw as the nature of post-capitalist society. She argued, first, for higher productivity: 'if production is to have the aim of securing for everyone a dignified life, plentiful food and providing other cultural means of existence, then the productivity of labor must be a great deal higher than it is now' (R: 346). Second, she argued that everyone must work: 'in order that everyone in society can enjoy prosperity, everybody must work.' There could be no scroungers and skivers: 'A life of leisure like most of the rich exploiters currently lead will come to an end' (R: 347).

Third, everyone must be engaged in useful employment that is committed to 'the general well-being'. Consequently, 'the entire war and munitions industries must be abolished' along with '[l]uxury industries which make all kinds of frippery for the idle rich', and the workers involved in these industries 'found more worthy and useful occupation'. Fourth, work must be organised in such a way as to ensure 'the health of the workforce and its enthusiasm for work': 'Short working hours that do not exceed the normal capability, healthy workrooms, all methods of recuperation and a variety of work must be introduced in order that everyone enjoys doing their part' (R: 347).

Finally, she insists that the new society calls not only for the end of the idleness of the rich – those who have lived off the surplus value provided by the labour of others – but for 'a complete inner rebirth of the proletarian':

> This calls for inner self-discipline, intellectual maturity, moral ardour, a sense of dignity and responsibility, a complete rebirth of the proletarian ... A socialist society needs human beings who, whatever their place, are full of passion and enthusiasm for the general well-being, full of self-sacrifice and sympathy for their fellow human beings, full of courage in order to dare to attempt the most difficult.
>
> (R: 348)

Implicit in this formulation of a new society is the assumption that, while economic freedom – the freedom from economic necessity and dependency – is a necessary condition of human agency, it is not in itself sufficient. Indeed, economic freedom in and of itself can all too easily reinforce the exploitative tendencies inherent in consumer capitalism.

What is needed is a notion of political freedom that includes both the economic and the social, and that – without any collapse into individualism – recognises the uniqueness of the individual agent within that economic and social nexus. We are, insisted Luxemburg, grounded in the social, which inflects on the one hand towards the reinforcement of its own norms and values while on the other hand offering the opportunity for oppositional pressure and resistance. In her posthumously published pamphlet, *The Russian Revolution*, written during her imprisonment in September 1918, she spelled out emphatically her notion of human freedom: 'Freedom is always and exclusively freedom for the one who thinks differently ... [A]ll that is instructive, wholesome and purifying in political freedom depends on this essential characteristic' (R: 305).

The spaces of freedom – the site of 'the political' – are both socialist spaces and democratic spaces. They are the spaces of protest and rebellion against injustice; they are inclusive spaces within which the experience of human suffering in all its forms is acknowledged and affirmed; they are spaces of unpredictability and surprise in which the impulse towards new meanings and values, new practices, new relationships and social formations finds collective expression. They are spaces in which, as Wolin puts it, democracy is reconceived as a means of gaining historical consciousness and of achieving political agency:

> Democracy needs to be reconceived ... as a mode of being which is conditioned by bitter experience, doomed to succeed only temporarily, but is a recurrent possibility as long as the memory of the political survives ... Democracy is a political moment, perhaps the political moment, when the political is remembered and recreated.
>
> (Wolin 2016: 111)

In his insistence on the democratic moment as *the* political moment – the moment at which the political is knowingly enacted – Wolin echoes one of Luxemburg's persistent themes: the indissoluble link between political action and the critical consciousness of the political agent.

4

Political Agency

Since André Gortz (1982) famously bade farewell to 'the working class' and proclaimed the arrival of 'the non-class post-industrial proletarians' as the new historical subject of the late twentieth century, there has been a burgeoning literature on the end of the industrial era and its impact on the labour market. We now live in a twenty-first century world where – a hundred years after Luxemburg's death – social class boundaries, global inequalities and demographic trends have shifted and re-rooted to such an extent that her assumptions regarding the underlying structure of society and the conditions necessary for radical change can seem hopelessly anachronistic. The tightly framed class structure she assumed – and her seeming assumption of the homogeneity of 'the working class' within that class structure – no longer reflect the reality of late capitalist and post-industrial societies characterised by cultural heterogeneity, the fragmentation of the labour market and deepening inequalities within and across generations (see, for example, Aronowitz and DeFazio 2010; Bluestone and Harrison 1984; Cowie 2012).

Within the UK – and the West generally – these changes are having a particular impact on the millennial generation: the 'Gen Y' of those born between 1980 and 1999. According to Mike Savage *et al.* (2015: 165–181), two major groups can be identified: an emergent 'technical middle class' and an increasingly disenfranchised 'precariat'. The former are under increasing pressure within a highly competitive and volatile labour market beset by graduate unemployment, while the latter are lucky to find any secure employment and are bearing the brunt of cut-backs in public expenditure. Both groups are – albeit in different ways and to a different extent – vulnerable to the pressures and tensions of what Erik Brynjolfsson and Andrew McAfee (2014) have termed late capitalism's 'second machine age', during which automation becomes an increasingly disruptive factor within the labour market. But neither group sits easily within a classificatory system that was designed to reflect the social and economic reality of 'the first machine age' (see also, Standing 2011).

Honneth identifies the general point at issue: 'Once the revolutionary proletariat disappeared and the industrial working class had become a minority among wage-workers, it became impossible to view socialist ideals as the intellectual expression of an already existing revolutionary subject' (2017: 41). In questioning the existence of 'an already existing revolutionary subject', Honneth raises some fundamental questions regarding the future of democratic socialism: if the 'revolutionary subject' is not 'already existing', how can we recognise it when we see it? Where might we look for it? How might we create the conditions necessary for its emergence and sustainability? Such questions lead to a radical redefinition not only of the 'revolutionary subject' but also of the organisational structures and systems that coalesce around that subject and create the conditions necessary for radical change.

Notwithstanding Luxemburg's regular references to 'the working class' and 'the proletariat', she provides a number of vital insights into how we might begin to address these questions in the here and now and for the future. First, she defines 'worker' so as to include within that category state employees such as army and naval personnel, railroad and postal workers, and those working outside the industrial sector. In her December 1918 address to the founding conference of the KPD, she was adamant that the council system should be expanded with a view not only to a broader geographical spread but also to greater inclusivity. She was particularly concerned that the council system was confined to urban areas and was committed to the expansion of that system to include agricultural workers ('we cannot bring about socialism without socialising agriculture') and the peasantry:

> there remains another important reserve which has not yet been taken into account: the peasantry ... Therefore, we have not merely to develop the system of workers' and soldiers' councils, but we

have to induce the agricultural laborers and the poorer peasants to adopt this council system.

(R: 370–371)

She was intent upon broadening the base of radical action.

Second, she insists on the need to reach across gender divides in order to fulfil the potential for radical change already contained within current society. One does not have to look to unrealized utopias to activate that potential. It exists in the here and now of everyday existence. Her close friend, Clara Zetkin was leader of the German Social Democratic Women's Movement and editor of *Gleichheit* (*'Equality'*). Luxemburg was heavily involved in women's issues, but there seems to have been an agreed division of labour between the two of them regarding their respective leadership roles within the various sections of the SPD and more broadly within the Second International. As and when required, Luxemburg spoke vehemently *against*, for example, the reformist-dominated Belgian Social Democrats for having agreed to drop their call for women's suffrage at the demand of the Liberals with which they were in coalition ('A Tactical Question', 1902) and the proposal that the women's association of the SPD should move to Brussels where the International Socialist Bureau was based, rather than remain in Stuttgart ('Address to the International Socialist Women's Conference', 1907) (see R: 233–242).

In her 1912 speech on 'Women's suffrage and class struggle', she spoke equally vehemently *for* the continuation of a working women's movement independent of the middle class German women's associations (R: 237–242). But her most unequivocal socialist feminist statement is contained in her article, 'Proletarian Women', written for International Women's Day, 8 March 1914, part of a week of demonstrations, meetings and recruitment known at the time as 'Red Week'. In this article, she places 'proletarian women' at the centre of revolutionary action: '*At the beginning of every social advance, there was the deed*. Proletarian women must gain solid ground in political life, through their activity in all areas; in this way alone will they secure a foundation for their rights.' The 'political demands' of 'the proletariat woman,' argues Luxemburg, 'are rooted deep in the social abyss that separates the class of the exploited from the class of the exploiters, not in the antagonism between man and woman but in the antagonism between capital and labor' (R: 242–244, emphasis in original).

Third, Luxemburg's analysis of the global effects of capitalist expansion shone a theoretical torchlight on hitherto largely forgotten areas of exploitation. Her mature work – in particular, her *Introduction to Political Economy* and *The Accumulation of Capital* – anticipated many of the themes that were later developed in the post-colonial critiques of, for example, Edward W. Said and Ahdaf Soueif and the exilic poetry and fiction of, among many others, Jamil Ahmed, Mahmoud Darwish and Danyal Mueenuddin (see Ahmad 2011; Darwish 2007; Mueenuddin 2010; Said, 1978; 1993; Soueif, 2004). The influence may be indirect, but it is there in the penumbra of their work. As John Berger – one of those who explicitly acknowledges his creative connection with the legacy of Luxemburg – puts it in his essay titled 'A Gift for Rosa Luxemburg':

> You often come out of a page I'm reading – and sometimes out of a page I'm trying to write – come out to join me with a toss of your head and a smile. No single page and none of the prison cells they repeatedly put you in could ever contain you.
>
> (Berger 2016: 87)

This international perspective gave to Luxemburg's work a deep sense of solidarity across national boundaries. The working class was, for her, an international movement of those who bore the brunt of nationalistic and imperialist expansion. The First World War was the perfect expression of the expansionist and nationalistic impulse lodged in the logic of capitalist accumulation: a fight to the death not between the national states of Europe but between those states and the cross-border proletariat who died in their hundreds of thousands in defence of a crumbling economic and political order. She stated her case with her usual vehemence and uncompromising rhetoric in the final paragraph of *The Junius Pamphlet*:

> This madness will not stop, and this bloody nightmare of hell will not cease until the workers of Germany, of France, of Russia and

of England will wake up out of their drunken sleep; will clasp each other's hands in brotherhood and will drown the bestial chorus of war agitators and the hoarse cry of capitalist hyenas with the mighty cry of labor: 'Proletarians of all countries, unite!'

(R: 341)

Luxemburg also glimpsed the ecological implications of her own economic analysis. Her responsiveness to the natural world is evident throughout her correspondence, as when, for example, she writes to Diefenbach from the fortress prison of Wronke (in a letter dated March 1917):

> How glad I am that three years ago I suddenly plunged into the study of botany the way I do everything, immediately, with all my fire and passion, with my entire being ... As a result I am now at home in the realm of greenery.
>
> (L: 386)

This sensitivity to the natural world gave her an acute sense of the impact of capitalist expansion on not only the human but also on the natural world. She saw that the human suffering resulting from that expansion is inextricably bound to the exploitation of the earth's natural resources. The revolutionary subject is thereby defined by her or his opposition to the impact of capitalist expansion on the human and natural world and by a shared sense of being in commonality with all those who – wherever and whenever – suffer the consequences of that exploitation.

Fourth – and crucially in respect of the major theme of this chapter – political agency is defined with reference not only to class position, but also to the agent's critical consciousness of the implications of her or his position. From Luxemburg's perspective, collective action springs from a critical understanding of the nature of exploitation and its differential impact on particular groups. That understanding is based on the experience of exploitation, but must be mediated through a process of critical consciousness, whereby one's own experience is understood within a broader social and economic totality. The political struggle is not located 'out there' in some autonomous political sphere, but is rooted in the critical consciousness of the political agent.

CRITICAL CONSCIOUSNESS

We can begin to understand what critical consciousness means by attending to the particular cast of mind reflected in Luxemburg's own work. Her writing falls into three broad categories: her political journalism and speeches, her theoretical work, and her vast correspondence. These vary in their style and content, but share a number of characteristics. They are, for example, intently communicative in that they involve a keen sense of the person or persons being addressed. In her letters, she addresses the immediate concerns of her correspondent as she understands them; in her polemics, she addresses her audience or readership directly and with a keen sense of their circumstances; and in her theoretical writing, which is necessarily pitched at a higher level of generality, she also engages directly and sometimes fiercely with her interlocutors. She never speaks or writes into a vacuum, but always with a particular person or persons in mind.

What Theodor Adorno wrote of the dialectic is a fitting description of Luxemburg's own mode of argument as developed in particular within her political pamphlets and speeches: 'the dialectic advances by way of extremes, driving thoughts with the utmost consequentiality to the point where they turn back on themselves, instead of qualifying them' ([1951] 2005: 86). She is always down there in the thick of the argument, employing every rhetorical device available to drive her point home. She is also a supremely expressive communicator who positions herself within her own argumentation and rhetoric. That is not to say that she invariably writes in the first person. Indeed, except in the more personal of her letters, she rarely employs that form. Her 'expressiveness' is of an entirely different order and, as Frölich suggests, is paradoxical in its simultaneous self-effacement and self-affirmation:

> the speaker faded almost completely into the background during the speech. Her ideas had such a strong riveting force that her listeners heard only the high, clear voice which expressed them,

until some particularly electrifying remark snapped them out of the spell. Nevertheless, it was the person, the compact personality behind the speech; the intense vigour; the harmony of feeling, purpose, and thought; the clarity, boldness, and aptness of her ideas; and the well-disciplined temperament which fascinated an audience.

(Frölich [1939] 2010: 197)

Somehow, suggests Frölich, Luxemburg manages to express herself – with great force and immediacy – without making her own self the object of expression.

In identifying the object of critical consciousness, Luxemburg placed great emphasis on the factual. Her detailed knowledge of the material conditions pertaining within successive economic systems informed both her understanding of political economy and the way in which she taught it: her lectures on political economy delivered at the SPD School in Berlin included detailed information on the price of slaves in ancient Rome, their clothing and shoes allowance, their monthly allowance of wheat, and the punishment regime to which they were subjected (CW I: 331–338). But the verifiable facts alone do not define the entirety of the object of critical inquiry. The social totality within which the verifiable facts are located, together with the perspective from they are identified and judged, are also of supreme importance.

It is with Luxemburg's emphasis on materialist knowledge as a key component of critical consciousness that we must begin, if we are to understand how she helped reconfigure the notion of political agency.

Materialist knowledge

The terms 'materialism' and 'materialist' carry considerable baggage. Williams provided a neat definition of the latter term when he suggested that 'it rests on a rejection of presumptive hypotheses of non-material or metaphysical prime causes, and defines its own categories in terms of demonstrable investigations' (1980: 103–104). But the problem, as he went on to argue, is that those categories can themselves become 'frozen forms' and assume the status of the 'presumptive hypotheses' that they originally opposed. The past is thereby reduced to a resource base for illustrating previously abstracted categories rather than for generating new and emergent hypotheses and questions. Political commitment, no less than material investigation, then 'finds itself stuck with its own recent generalizations', some of which may not have fully embedded themselves within the dominant discourse and therefore may be difficult to identify. Collective action – premised, as Luxemburg maintains, on critical consciousness – is then blocked.

Luxemburg was well aware of this problem of cultural sedimentation whereby 'recent generalizations' and 'frozen forms' constitute an enduring ideological residue. Indeed, it was one of the main reasons that she was at odds not only with the revisionists within the SPD but also with those of her fellow Marxists who sought to entrench Marxism as an orthodoxy. For Luxemburg, Marxism was a living tradition within which knowledge is grounded in the material world and in which materialist knowledge is rooted in the historical: rooted not in a linear chronology into which past events can be neatly slotted with the wisdom of hindsight, but in a dynamic historical process whereby past events are constantly reinterpreted as their consequences erupt in the present and reshape our sense of future possibilities. By looking at the actual power relations in play within historically located economic systems – notably those associated with primitive, ancient, feudal, pre-capitalist and capitalist societies – she was able to identify and challenge a number of 'recent generalisations' and 'frozen forms' that, in her view, blocked the possibility of collective action through a process of mystification, or, more simply, not telling it as it is.

In her 1899 *Social Reform or Revolution*, she had mounted a fierce attack on the reformist agenda and one of its 'recent generalisations' that history reveals a grand narrative of human progress and perfectibility within which a reformed version of capitalism is – potentially at least – the triumphant finale. Through her political analysis of the economic systems developed within successive eras she sought to show, notably in her *Introduction to Political Economy*, that dissolution as opposed to progress was central to each of those specific systems: the erosion of communal bonds led to the dissolution of early primitive societies; slavery undermined the economic viability of ancient Greece and Rome and ultimately led to their demise; the consolidation of private property around particular patriarchal interests led to the implosion of feudal societies within the European Middle Ages; and pre-capitalist societies – engulfed by the expansionist logic of capitalist accumulation – were subject to relentless colonisation and exploitation. The long saga of dissolution then reaches its denouement. As non-capitalist resources are systematically depleted, the potential for capitalist expansion is inevitably exhausted. Capitalism falls victim to its own rapacity.

A lingering assumption – or 'frozen form' – in Marxist circles was that following the final conflagration of capitalism socialism would inevitably rise phoenix-like from the flames. Luxemburg had always challenged the implicit complacency of this assumption. But the inescapable factuality of the First World War – and her outrage at the support given by the SPD to the war effort – confirmed her in her long-held belief that there was nothing inevitable about the emergence of socialism. On the contrary, global barbarism was – as she spelled out in *The Junius Pamphlet* – the inevitable consequence of an imperialist war that was engulfing Europe and the consequences of which were being experienced far beyond the continent:

> *This world war* means a reversion to barbarism. The triumph of imperialism leads to the destruction of culture, sporadically during a modern war, and forever, if the period of world wars that has just begun is allowed to take its damnable course to the last ultimate consequence.
>
> (R: 321, emphasis in original)

The only alternative to 'the triumph of imperialism and the destruction of all culture' is 'the conscious struggle of the international proletariat against imperialism, against its methods, against war' (R: 321).

The barbarity of war – both in anticipation and in reality – produced an overriding sense of hopelessness, to which Luxemburg was herself not immune. Her despair – and outrage – at the failure of the SPD to resist the relentless march of events that culminated in war was acute. The generalised feeling that modernity was an encounter with 'the horror' (as depicted in Joseph Conrad's 1899 *Heart of Darkness*) and that European civilisation had been reduced to 'fear in a handful of dust' (as T.S. Eliot suggested in his 1922 *The Wasteland*) was shaping and informing a new kind of cultural pessimism. Luxemburg never directly confronted what we now think of as 'modernism' (she was murdered while it was still emerging as the dominant artistic and literary movement of the early twentieth century). But her involvement in the early days of the German Revolution was an emphatic rebuttal of the nihilism that characterised some – but by no means all – modernist art and literature. Luxemburg was here challenging one of the emergent formulations that would shape the decade following her murder – *l'entre deux guerres* – and constitute a part at least of that decade's cultural legacy. In her final piece for *Die Rote Fahne*, she made it absolutely clear that the undeniable fact of resistance was a bulwark against any form of nihilism: 'Immediate resistance came forth spontaneously from the masses of Berlin with such an obvious energy that from the very beginning the moral victory was on the side of the "street"' (R: 376).

We cannot – and should not – infer from Luxemburg's mode of analysis that knowledge is unmediated by concepts, presuppositions and prior understandings. On the contrary, her work shows how knowledge is constantly filtered through a web of ideas, many of which we simply take for granted. It is for that reason that Luxemburg insists on the need to subject those ideas to critical scrutiny through what Williams called 'demonstrable investigations'. Some of those ideas, she found illuminating, including much of the conceptual framework provided by Marxism. But others, she rejected on the grounds that they avoided, distorted or prevented a genuine understanding of the material conditions pertaining within particular economic systems. They mystified rather than enlightened. She understood, as Nye puts it, that '[m]aterialism ... is the study and analysis of actual material conditions which are bound to change' (1994: 50). It is because they are 'bound to change' that the generalisations – or hypotheses – we derive from them need to be constantly questioned, revised and rethought.

Social totality

If one of the lessons of Luxemburg's thought is an unswerving attention to the particularity of the material conditions pertaining within different economic systems, another is the need to grasp, along with the particular facts, the whole of the ideological forces that hold those particulars in place. At one level, this involves grasping the interconnectivity of events across spatial expanses and across time: the connection, for example, between the growth of cotton mills in England, the expansion of the African slave trade, and the price rises and resultant famines in South-East Asia. In shifting the object of analysis from the workings of the national economy to the operation of not only a global but an imperially expansionist economy, Luxemburg was broadening the analytical frame. The economic thesis she was advancing required a mode of analysis that looked to the spaces *between* the particular facts and sought to uncover hidden or partially revealed causalities and effects. At a fairly simple level of methodological procedure, the material conditions in one country or region had therefore to be seen as having a bearing on those in other countries and regions.

But because she was focusing not on the economy as a dis-embedded system but also on the global economy as embedded within particular cultural and social contexts, she was – at a more sophisticated level – primarily concerned with the forces that shaped and drove these global interconnectivities: forces that lie outside the descriptive frame of comparative economics. Marxism had traditionally explained those forces in terms of a determining economic base and a determined superstructure. Luxemburg understood that this formulation was too static in its assumption of a fixed and generalised hierarchy of determination. She insisted therefore not only on the interconnectivities operating across national regions, but on the dynamic relation between the cultural, economic and social factors operating on and shaping the material conditions pertaining within particular societies at particular times. She was searching for a notion of totality that acknowledged the dynamic interrelation of those factors within and across geographically and historically grounded localities.

In doing so, she was anticipating Antonio Gramsci's emphasis on 'hegemony' as something that is not merely superstructural, but that is truly total in the sense that it saturates the whole of the social and economic order and constitutes the substance and limits of common sense. Hegemony, argued Gramsci functions by domination through consent: '[t]he "spontaneous" consent given by the great masses of the population to the general direction imposed on social life by the dominant fundamental group' (1971: 12). Luxemburg did not theorise domination in quite these terms, but she clearly understood how consent and acquiescence are key elements in the machinery of domination. That is why, in her address to the founding conference of the KPD, she insisted that one of the prime tasks facing the party was to raise the consciousness of those who had joined the workers' and soldiers' councils:

> the members of our own Party and the proletarians in general must be educated. Even where workers' and soldiers' councils already exist, there is still a lack of consciousness of the purposes for which they exist. We must make the masses understand that the workers' and soldiers' council is in all senses the lever of the machinery of state, that it must take over all power and must unify the power in one stream – the socialist revolution.
>
> (R: 372)

Only by refusing to acquiesce to the manipulations and blandishments of the Ebert–Scheidemann government could the councils begin to constitute an effective counter-hegemonic bloc.

She also understood that we are all part of the hegemonic totality that she identified as a crucial element in the revolutionary politics of her own period and that was one of the defining features of the phase of capitalism that followed the First World War: the collapse into the twin totalitarianisms of Nazism and Stalinism and the emergence of what Wolin (2010) described as 'the specter of inverted totalitarianism' that characterised the neoliberal order of the late twentieth century as it toppled over into the global economic crisis of 2007–2008. There is no *deus ex machina* to lift us out of the complex and multi-layered totality of which we are a part; no *primum mobile* to explain by a process of infinite regression why we are where we are; no *archimedian point* from which to gain external leverage other than our own capacity for human action. We achieve agency not by attempting – in vain – to achieve a neutral or outsider perspective on history, but by acknowledging that we are a part of history and that in order to remake it we need to understand our potentially revolutionary role within it.

Critical consciousness and political agency are inevitably intertwined. Action flows from my own understanding, not from any understanding that is imposed upon me by 'the machinery of state' – or, indeed, any kind of vanguard, party or clique that assumes to represent my class interests. That is why Luxemburg insisted that '[t]he masses must learn to use power by using power'. Power means *empowerment*, which is achieved through a critical awareness of how domination operates within the social totality. We achieve that awareness, insists Luxemburg, by trial and error, feeling our way into action, pulling back and taking stock, moving forward 'step by step'. No one can do that alone, but nor can anyone or any group do it for us. We must do it for ourselves. That is the crux of Luxemburg's democratic socialism: power cannot be gained by proxy. It is achieved through collective action.

The primacy of perspective

But we have to choose how to deploy that power: with whom to act and to what end. Our politics are defined not by our given class position, but by the critical consciousness which arises from the particular perspective we choose to adopt. Perspective is political – or, rather, our choice of perspective is a political act. Our angle of vision affects not only what we see, but the social and political context within which it is framed – an insight that the Austrian journalist, writer and politician Ernst Fischer developed as one of the central themes of his seminal *The Necessity of Art* (1959): 'Subject is raised to the status of content only by the artist's attitude, for content is not only *what* is presented but also *how* it is presented, in what context, with what degree of social and individual consciousness'. *How* it is presented is, therefore, a matter of political choice: 'everything depends on the artist's view, on whether he speaks as an apologist of the ruling class, a sentimental Sunday tripper, a disgruntled peasant, or a revolutionary socialist' (Fischer [1959] 2010: 149, emphasis in original).

'Viewpoint' is the main focus of Luxemburg's critique of Bernstein, whose theorising, she argued, developed entirely from the viewpoint of 'the individual capitalist': 'Bernstein's theory of adaptation is nothing but a theoretical generalization of the conception of the individual capitalist. What is this viewpoint theoretically if not the essential and characteristic aspect of our bourgeois vulgar economics?' Given his 'viewpoint', Bernstein was incapable of grasping the full impact of 'the whole capitalist economy' on individual lives and communities: 'All the economic errors of this school rest precisely on the conception that mistakes the phenomenon of competition, as seen from the angle of the individual capitalist, for the phenomenon of the whole capitalist economy'. As a result, argues Luxemburg, he considers the recurring 'crises' of capitalism: 'to be simple "derangements" or simple "means of adaptation" ... [and] ends up with a reactionary and not a revolutionary program, and thus in a utopia'. Bernstein's viewpoint not only limits but also severely distorts his notion of 'the whole capitalist economy' (R: 145).

What Bernstein lacked, in Luxemburg's view, was the critical consciousness necessary to see beyond the interests of 'the individual capitalist'. That was partly because, as she made clear in *Social Reform or Socialism*, he had failed to take full account of the impact of the global capitalist economy on the material conditions of the working class and the non-capitalist regions upon which capitalism relied for its natural resources, labour and emergent markets. It was also partly because he failed to appreciate the extent to which this impact involved not only the economic but also the whole way of life of individuals and communities within a complex and dynamic social totality. But it was, also, because his arguments failed to reflect one of the qualities that Luxemburg possessed in abundance, namely, a deep humanism that sprang directly from her insistence in standing alongside the international proletariat and analysing the workings of global capitalism from their perspective.

This humanistic impulse is evident throughout her life and work, but is particularly apparent in her emphasis on reclaiming the lost or forgotten histories of human struggle and human suffering. In this respect, she undoubtedly fulfilled Said's requirements regarding 'the intellectual's role' as being 'to present alternative narratives and other perspectives on history than those provided by combatants on behalf of official memory and national identity and mission' (2004: 141). She pitted her wide ranging historical analyses against what Said goes on to describe as 'the invidious disfiguring, dismembering, and disremembering of significant historical experiences that do not have powerful enough lobbies in the present and therefore merit dismissal or belittlement' (2004: 141).

Indeed, the charge she levels against Kautsky is precisely that of 'disfiguring, dismembering, and disremembering' the past:

> To derive the mass strike action of the Russian proletariat, unparalleled in the history of modern class struggle, from Russia's social backwardness ...; to explain the outstanding importance and leading role of the of the urban industrial proletariat in the Russian Revolution as Russian 'backwardness' – is to stand things right on their heads.
>
> (R: 224)

Kautsky's theorising is false 'from the ground up', as she puts it, because he had disremembered the enormous potential of the proletariat and in so doing disfigured it. Like Bernstein, he had seen only what he wanted to see and at the angle from which he wanted to see it – and ended up with 'a blooming fantasy' (R: 216).

For Luxemburg, the potential of the proletariat was the cornerstone of democratic socialism. '[D]emocracy is indispensable,' she wrote in her riposte to Bernstein, 'not because it renders *superfluous* the conquest of political power by the proletariat but, on the contrary, because it renders this conquest of power both *necessary* as well as *possible*' (R: 157, emphasis in original). Luxemburg was able to perceive that necessity and grasp that possibility because her notion of democracy was informed by her critical consciousness of the exploitative nature of global capitalism and of its destructive impact on individual lives and communities. She saw the world from the perspective of those who endured the injustices of capitalism and whose political agency was realized through their struggle against those injustices. They, for Luxemburg, constituted the revolutionary subject.

CRITICAL IMAGINARIES

How might we characterise the political agent as imagined by Luxemburg? If, to return to Honneth, it has become impossible to view socialism as the expression of an *already existing* revolutionary subject, then what might the new or emergent revolutionary subject look like? To broaden the question: how does critical consciousness manifest itself within a post-industrial and late-capitalist society, typified by escalating inequalities within and across nation states, the increasing power and influence of new global elites, and the relentless rise of the homeless and stateless escaping persecution, poverty, torture and war? How – in these unpropitious circumstances – are we to identify the revolutionary subject?

We know, from how Luxemburg lived and from what she wrote, that revolutionary subjects operate collectively and collaboratively; that the freedom to which they aspire lies in their capacity to think differently while thinking together; that they constitute neither an atomised nor a homogenous mass. They are individuals who delight in their individuality while spurning individualism; they are comrades who delight in solidarity while rejecting any notion of exclusivity. Their councils – collectivities, groupings, formations – are inclusive and outward looking. No one is defined solely by party affiliation. Negotiation, argument and disagreement are their ways of working together. No one – under any circumstances – says: 'I am not interested in your opinion'. Engagement, critique and dialogue are all-important.

We know also that revolutionary subjects as conceived by Luxemburg are endlessly curious regarding the material conditions of people's lives. They start with facts, not with ideologies or tribal loyalties: facts that tell the previously untold stories; give the lie to the half-truths and untruths of official narratives; confront the dominant ideologies of the day. They see one of their prime tasks as being to communicate those facts, disseminate them and gather them into counter-analyses. They are intent upon producing *useful* knowledge. Their ideas – because they love ideas – are always grounded in the facts as they relate to specific contexts. The facts bring those contexts to life – in all their rich social totality – through imagery, storytelling and reportage. Like Luxemburg, the revolutionary subject is enthralled by the particularity of things.

She – the revolutionary subject – is also enthralled by their interconnectivity and interdependency: the way things hang together and fall apart. She is an internationalist to the roots of her being. We might describe her as 'cosmopolitan', provided we define 'cosmopolitanism' – in the terms used by Kwame Anthony Appiah – as 'rooted' and 'tenable': 'rooted' in the sense of the global being grounded in the local; 'tenable' in the sense of the local being held within the global (2005: 213–272). 'A tenable cosmopolitanism,' writes Appiah, 'must take seriously the value of human life, and the value of particular human lives, the lives people have made for themselves, within the communities that help lend significance to those lives' (Appiah 2005: 222–223). The revolutionary subject applies the universal values of international solidarity at precise points and within specific sectors. She knows that it is at those precise points and within those specific sectors that change can be brought about.

The revolutionary subject believes that education is potentially emancipatory insofar as it informs, extends horizons and provides the tools for critical analysis. She knows that education is lifelong, occurs in a multitude of formal and informal settings, and is grounded in common understandings and shared meanings. She recognises, as Williams expresses it, that 'education is ordinary' (1989: 14). Where and when necessary, she takes responsibility for establishing new educational forums, sites and networks – as Luxemburg did in helping establish the SPD School in Berlin. In the 1950s and 1960s, she set up Saturday Schools and Supplementary Schools for the newly arrived black British; in the second decade of the twenty-first century, she has established outposts of learning in the refugee camps staggered across the Mediterranean; she continues to blog, network, broadcast and – crucially – bring people together. She is indefatigable in her insistence on the power of education to empower.

We can recognise the revolutionary subject as conceived by Luxemburg by what she attends to and how she attends to it. As Luxemburg illustrated, it is sometimes – under certain circumstances – revolutionary to attend to the plight of a frozen bumblebee. Revolution resides in particularity not generality – and in the quality of our attention to the specificity of suffering. The crucial point is to understand the ostensible world from the perspective of its often hidden underside and, in so doing, stand alongside those who constitute that underside. Luxemburg never claimed to be a representative of – or spokesperson for – 'the masses'. Her words never sought to colonise their causes or their anger. She simply stood by them, using the resources available to her in order to help realize their potential for critical consciousness and their capacity for political agency.

To be fully conscious involves having an imaginative grasp of what might have been and what might be; what needs reclaiming and what needs reimagining; what should be exposed as enduring falsehoods and what should be affirmed as new and emergent possibilities. 'For Luxemburg,' writes Jacqueline Rose, 'there is no politics without a poetics of revolution. If you want to understand the revolution, look to the stars' (2011: 6). Rose is here referring to the stars that Luxemburg viewed from the window of her prison cell, but we might also think of them as the stars that for Luxemburg were reflected in the everyday and the ordinary. It was always in the here and now – and step by step – that Luxemburg discovered her political ends and purposes.

5
Political Purpose

History, maintained Luxemburg, is open and indeterminate. It cannot be defined in terms of predetermined outcomes. Our distant ends and purposes come into view only slowly and intermittently, as we move towards them 'step by step'. Each action is a new step taken and each new step taken is an opportunity to take stock, reconsider our options and work out the next step. Our actions – and our response to the consequences of those actions – clarify and articulate our ends and purposes, as we move gradually towards their realization: a process that is both heuristic in its re-evaluation of those ends and purposes and anticipatory of their final realization.

This emphasis on the indeterminacy of history and the formative nature of political purpose lies at the heart of Luxemburg's critical reflections on 'Spartacus Week'. As she argued at the founding conference of the KPD, the events of that week and the weeks leading up to it represented neither a final victory nor a final defeat. The events failed to bring about regime change, but – as she put it in her 11 January letter to Clara Zetkin – they nevertheless constituted 'a tremendous school for the masses' (L: 492). 'Spartacus Week', Luxemburg maintained, had symbolic value as an act of collective resistance to state violence, while also providing important lessons in the need to revitalise and extend the network of workers' and soldiers' councils. She concluded her speech to the delegates of that conference with the hope that her 'description of the difficulties of the accumulating tasks will paralyze neither your zeal nor your energy' (R: 373). 'Spartacus Week' may have exposed serious weaknesses in the revolutionary movement, but it also reasserted the willingness of that movement to take a stance and in so doing reaffirm its commitment to the ends and purposes of revolutionary action.

Judged against their ultimate ends and purposes all revolutionary acts might be said to be 'premature': a point which Bernstein attempted to use against Luxemburg's support for mass action. Luxemburg's response as developed in her 1899 *Social Reform or Revolution* was to counter Bernstein's accusation with arguments based on the nature of 'socialist transformation':

> The socialist transformation presupposes a long and stubborn struggle in the course of which, quite probably, the proletariat will be repulsed more than once, so that, from the viewpoint of the final outcome of the struggle, it will have necessarily come to power 'too early' the first time.
>
> (R: 159)

She continues:

> Since the proletariat is absolutely obliged to seize power 'too early' once or several times before it can enduringly maintain itself in power, the objection to *'premature'* seizure of power is nothing other than a *general opposition to the aspiration of the proletariat to take state power.*
>
> (R: 159, emphasis in original).

Bernstein's supposedly pragmatic objection to mass action on the grounds of its lack of timeliness is, claims Luxemburg, merely a cover for his underlying opposition to its ultimate ends and purposes.

Commenting on this particular passage in *Social Reform or Revolution*, the Slovenian-born philosopher Slavoj Žižek writes:

> There is no ... outside position from which the agent can calculate how many 'premature' attempts are needed to get at the right moment ... [A]n act always occurs simultaneously too fast ... and too late ... In short, *there is no right moment to act.*
>
> (Žižek 2014: 113–114, emphasis in original).

An act is always 'too fast' because, as he puts it, 'the act has to anticipate its certainty and risk that it will retroactively establish its own conditions'; it is always 'too late' because 'every act is a reaction to circumstances which arose because we were too late to act.' Action, maintains Žižek, is located in this betwixt and between space of uncertainty and unpredictability.

Luxemburg is of course referring to a particular kind of action that is both collective and purposeful: collective in the sense that it involves shared purposes and purposeful in the sense that each individual is personally committed to those purposes. It combines solidarity with individual agency. Such action is wholly different from the routinised behaviour associated with the kind of capitalist mode of production in which each step is programmed and predetermined and where the person performing the routine actions has no personal investment in the 'final outcome'. Luxemburg understood that if 'the socialist transformation' was to be worked through at the level of practice, then any attempt to programme or predetermine the collective action of the proletariat would have to be fiercely resisted. The ends and purposes of that transformation would have to be shaped by the actions of those engaged in and immediately affected by that transformation – *not* by any political party or intellectual vanguard acting on their behalf.

The distinction between routinised behaviour and transformative action and the emphasis on the unpredictability of the latter marks a significant line of continuity between Luxemburg's political thought in the early twentieth century and that of Arendt in the mid-twentieth century. Central to Arendt's argument in her 1958 *The Human Condition* is her insistence on the need to acknowledge both our human agency and our commonality: 'nobody is the author or producer of his own life story ... [T]he stories, the results of action and speech, reveal an agent, but this agent is not an author or producer' (Arendt [1958] 1998: 184). We cannot write the script in advance – nor can anyone write it for us – since the consequences of our words and actions are both unpredictable and irreversible. The consequences cannot be predicted let alone predetermined. Only by acting together – and proceeding 'step by step' – can we begin to take control of the flux and uncertainty of the human condition and gain a sense of common purpose.

For Luxemburg, what is 'revolutionary' about 'revolution' is neither the bloodshed (which may nevertheless be one of its consequences) nor the individual and collective acts of courage and self-sacrifice (which are certain to be among the consequences), but the constitution of a new economic, political and social order. Luxemburg was arguing for a historically distinct kind of revolution – a revolution generated and led not by an emergent middle class or an intellectual elite, but by a historically exploited working class that was economically, politically and socially trapped within a system of capitalist exploitation. Only by acting together – and in full consciousness of the conditions requiring collective action – could that potentially powerful group realize its collective agency.

ENDS AND PURPOSES

Revolution – or, indeed, any great political transformation – involves two impulses: *freedom from* an existing order; and *freedom to* create a new order. While these two impulses vie for ascendancy within any transformational movement, the final end of revolutionary action is the latter rather than the former. So each step on the way must involve a re-commitment to that final end – a re-commitment which involves moving forward in anticipation of an order that can only be inferred from the emergent and pre-emergent revolutionary elements within the existing order. As Geras argues, this notion of the past weighing upon the future is central to Luxemburg's thinking:

> For Rosa Luxemburg, the socialist revolution … cannot pay homage only to its *telos*. In some measure, but, all the same, inevitably, it is also governed by the reality it undertakes to destroy. It is marked, *irredeemably*, by its beginning as well as by its end.
>
> (Geras [1976] 2015: 164, emphasis in original).

Benjamin, in the second of his 'Theses on the Philosophy of History' (completed in spring 1940), also emphasises the power of the past over the present, as it topples into the future. But he sees the revolutionary act not as irredeemably marked by the past, but as the retroactive redemption of past failed acts:

The past carries with it a temporal index by which it is referred to redemption. There is a secret agreement between past generations and the present one. Our coming was expected on earth. Like every generation that preceded us, we have been endowed with a *weak* Messianic power, a power to which the past has a claim. That claim cannot be settled cheaply.

(Benjamin [1968] 2007: 254, emphasis in original)

Revolutionary action is an attempt to settle the claim that the past has on the present. It plays back upon the past – as reinterpretation, historical recovery and reclamation, and the upsurge of latent energy – while playing forward into the future.

Collective action that ignored – or was ignorant of – what Geras called 'the reality it undertakes to destroy' would end in an unrealized utopia; conversely, collective action that was unable to think beyond the destruction of that reality might well end in an all too real dystopia. Luxemburg's message is unequivocal: without the critical consciousness necessary to understand what is being *fought against* and what is being *fought for*, any attempt at revolutionary action will inevitably fail. Purposeful action requires critical consciousness; critical consciousness requires materialist knowledge; and materialist knowledge requires the perspective of the oppressed and the exploited. As she wrote in a text titled *Slavery*, drafted for the SPD School in Berlin: 'In the socialist society, knowledge will be the common property of everyone. All working people will have knowledge' (R: 122).

But knowledge does not in itself constitute critical consciousness. Luxemburg constantly reminds us of the need to use knowledge for the purpose of criticism and self-criticism and with a view to informing our actions and our response to the consequences of those actions. Her unique contribution to the understanding of revolutionary action lies in her insistence on the indispensable complementarity of collective action and critical consciousness. 'In the beginning was the deed,' she declared (R: 255) – but 'the deed', as she also affirmed, carries with it unforeseeable consequences that must be gathered into a new order of democratic organisation.

The deed

In emphasising the 'spontaneity' of revolutionary action, Luxemburg is rejecting traditional forms of organisation and planning associated with the old order that such action seeks to overturn. But she is also affirming her belief that such action has the potential for generating alternative forms of organisation and planning that crystallise around the collective will and critical consciousness of the participants and thereby anticipate the establishment of an alternative order. At issue was the overall control of the collective action, the organisational structure within which the collective action unfolds, and the *telos* or end point of action. Underlying these crucial issues was a further issue regarding the basis upon which a democratically socialist solidarity might be founded.

Luxemburg was rejecting a mode of organisation that relied on external control, hierarchical structure and the pre-specification of operational goals. Since these organisational mechanisms reproduced the old order of power and control, their adoption was counter to the final ends and purposes of the socialist revolution. '[G]reat movements of the people', she argued in *The Junius Pamphlet*, 'are not produced according to technical recipes that repose in the pockets of the party leaders' (R: 308). What she was affirming was an order of power and control based upon a very different relation between organisation and struggle. She maintained that revolutionary action should be generated from below, that it should be led from within decentralised and locally based units of operation, and that it should be flexible and responsive to the rapidly changing circumstances pertaining in any revolutionary or potentially revolutionary situation. She was arguing for a solidarity of purpose that focuses on 'the deed' rather than a solidarity of assent and obedience.

For the French philosopher Alain Badiou, 'the deed' – or, to employ his own terminology, 'the event' – is centrally concerned with the opening-up of possibility:

> an event is something that brings to light a possibility that was invisible or even unthinkable. An event is not by itself the creation of a reality; it is the creation of a possibility, it opens up a

possibility. It indicates to us that a possibility exists that has been ignored. The event is, in a certain way, merely a proposition. It proposes something to us. Everything will depend on the way in which the possibility proposed by the event is grasped, elaborated, incorporated and set out in the world.

(Badiou 2013: 9–10)

Power, argues Badiou, resides with those who claim to have the monopoly of possibilities: 'what pronounces that which is possible and impossible'. With what he calls 'a political event, a possibility emerges that escapes the prevailing power's control over possibles.' When this happens, claims Badiou,

All of a sudden people, sometimes masses of people, start to think there is another possibility. They gather together to discuss it, they form new organizations. They make some immense errors but that's not the important point. They make the possibility opened up by the event come alive … The event, for its part, will transform what has been declared impossible into a possibility. The possible will be wrested from the impossible.

(Badiou 2013: 11)

Badiou here clearly reflects something of the revolutionary fervour that Luxemburg sought to convey when she declared in her speech to the founding conference of the KPD: 'Our motto is: In the beginning was the act' (R: 372). We can also grasp in that declaration clear echoes of the Egyptian uprising in Cairo's Tahrir Square: 'Did we not,' asks Žižek 'encounter something of the same order when, in 2011, we followed with enthusiasm the Egyptian uprising in Cairo's Tahrir Square?' (Žižek 2014: 84). Those who are sceptical of the revolutionary significance of that uprising, he claims,

are blind to the 'miraculous' nature of the events in Egypt: something happened that few people predicted, violating the experts' opinions, as if the uprising was not simply the result of social causes but of the intervention of a foreign agency into history.

(Žižek 2014: 84)

That agency, he claims, is the 'Eternal Idea of freedom, justice and dignity' (see also Bassiouni 2016; Iskandar 2013).

Although Luxemburg may not have categorised freedom, justice and dignity as an 'Eternal Idea', she would undoubtedly have recognised and indeed warmed to the idea of them erupting into history through the political agency of men and women intent upon wresting the possible from the impossible – and doing so both in their everyday lives and in the broader social and political structures within which they coexist. But she would also have set alongside that recognition her acute awareness of the *experience* of revolutionary action: its muddle and confusion, its sense of unresolved struggle, its messiness. 'Everything,' as she wrote to her friend and fellow Spartacist, Mehring, in August 1915, 'is still in the process of moving and shifting, and the giant landslide seems to have no end whatever, and on such churned-up and fluctuating ground it is a devilishly difficult task to decide strategy and organize the battle' (R: 351).

'The readiness is all'

How, then, 'on such churned-up and fluctuating ground', can one prepare for 'the deed'? Part of an answer to that question, insists Luxemburg, is to be found in the state of mind of the participants: to be prepared is to be aware that the prevailing powers do not have absolute control of the possibilities and to be conscious of one's own countervailing power to seize the opportunities opened up by those possibilities. Just as the action shapes the organisational structure, so the state of consciousness creates the conditions necessary for the action and, therefore, in its own turn shapes history. As Hamlet, prior to the climactic showdown that was to end his own life and that of the ruling regime, commented: 'the readiness is all'.

Badiou's comments are again helpful in this respect and reflect Luxemburg's own lifelong preoccupations and priorities. He offers two responses to the question, 'How, then, should you prepare yourself?' His first response is 'remaining faithful to a past event'. Political subjects, he argues, are always between the past event and the coming event: 'They are never simply confronted with the opposition between the event and the situation but are in a situation upon which events of the recent or distant past still have an impact' (2013: 13–14). The coming event – burdened with its own 'prematurity' – only makes sense as part of a temporal sequence that includes fidelity to past ('premature') events. Purposefulness is about the connectivity of events, which – in retrospect – form a pattern, tell a story, provide hope. The prematurity of action grasped in hindsight reveals purposefulness.

Luxemburg is continually reminding her readers, her audiences and, indeed, herself of the revolutionary tradition within which their collective action achieves significance and to which it contributes energy and momentum. From the perspective of those who control the narrative, the revolutionary past is systematically portrayed as a sequence of unremitting defeats. But, she insists, from an alternative perspective those defeats build towards something very different: not an apocalyptic victory but the steady and purposeful formation of democratic socialism both within the consciousness of people and within the culture and social structures that they inhabit. That process of 'Bildung' or cultural formation – the gathering of the resources of the past into the present and the carrying forward of those resources into the future – is central to Luxemburg's notion of preparedness.

Badiou's second response to the question he poses – 'How, then, should you prepare yourself?' – is 'criticism of the established order'. The critical task, he argues, lies in showing that the system of possibilities on offer is 'ultimately inhuman': 'this system does not propose to the social collectivity, to living humanity, possibilities that do justice to that of which it is capable'. This is not a system that is part of the natural order of things, but a system that is purposefully constructed and must therefore be purposefully resisted. Moreover, it must be resisted in the interests not of an ideology or a party or a faction, but in the cause of 'living humanity'. To wilfully restrict human possibility is to deny humanity. This, crucially, is the point at which socialism, democracy and humanism interconnect.

Luxemburg was acutely aware of the dehumanising effects of capitalism and of the need for a re-humanising vision that opened up the possibilities for men and women, and that did so by challenging a system that was economically exploitative, socially divisive and culturally oppressive. The SPD School in Berlin, which Luxemburg taught in, developed and defended is crucial in this respect. Her aim was to develop a cadre of activists from across the regions, who – using their own knowledge of their own localities – could build on the analytical frameworks, which she developed in the course of her teaching. She was in effect building a common culture, a shared critical heritage, and an embryonic polity from which a politics of new possibilities might take root.

'She was,' as Paul Levi put it in his memorial address delivered in the Teachers Union building in Berlin on 2 February 1919, 'the best teacher, she was the leading theoretical mind and temperament.' Levi continued:

> I believe there was scarcely a more pleasant memory in Rosa Luxemburg's life than in 1913 when Eduard Bernstein sought to have her dismissed from this post. Man for man (these were grown-up students), whether they remained her supporters or subsequently turned against her, the students supported Rosa Luxemburg and gave such testimony for her that even a German party leadership had to abandon the idea of dismissing her.
>
> (quoted in Jacob 2000: 122)

This commitment to building communities of shared critical understanding and practice was central to Luxemburg's politics. How – together – can ordinary people caught up in extraordinary circumstances seek to change not only their own situation but also the situation of those around them and of those in the wider world? That was, for her, the crucial question. She understood from an early age that the world was upside down. 'Socialists are not in the least thinking of turning the world upside down,' she declared in 1900, 'for it is upside down already' (RPL: 42). Her doctoral thesis was based on precisely that assumption: capital accumulation constituted a social and economic pyramid at the apex of which resided the capitalists and profiteers, the beneficiaries of accumulated wealth, and the upholders of entrenched privilege.

But she also grew into an understanding of how the world had to be turned the right way up – not only in its economic, social and civic structures, but in our consciousness of those structures – and that this overturning of the world could only be achieved through collective understanding and collective action: an approach to action and understanding based on an ethics of magnanimity.

The ethical bases

Political purposefulness – as conceived by Luxemburg – constitutes a cyclical process: critical consciousness leads to collective action, which in turn leads to new and emergent forms of social organisation, which further expand the horizons of critical consciousness, thereby providing the impetus for renewed action. But this is not a self-enclosed and self-perpetuating system. On the contrary, its momentum is sustained and informed at every phase through its responsiveness to new ideas and practices, new constituencies and social groupings, new and experimental ways of working together. Political purposes achieve fulfilment not only through collective consciousness, collective action and collective organisation, but also through an approach to collective practice that is inclusive, expansive and magnanimous. That is why purposes always reach beyond whatever end is defined as their point of eventual closure.

Luxemburg – in her life and in her work – was constantly reaching out in her thinking and her political practice and encouraging others to do likewise. Her notion of critical consciousness – and her own deployment of this faculty – reveals the importance of understanding how global capitalism impacts on capitalist and pre-capitalist societies and how the voices of those who suffer the deleterious impact of global capitalism inform that critical consciousness. She was also aware that while individual action may be a requirement of individual human agency, collective action is a necessary requirement of political power. Solidarity is all well and good, but the quality of that solidarity depends upon its inclusivity: not an inclusivity of 'anything goes' but an inclusivity that requires ongoing deliberation as to where the boundaries lie and who should determine them. Both the critical consciousness that drives revolutionary action and the collective nature of that action rely on inclusive ways of thinking together and working together.

These ways of thinking and working together are also crucial to how organisation coalesces – or, to use Luxemburg's image, crystallises – around action: how form flows from action and how action gains a sense of direction and cohesion from how its consequences are understood in the process of their unfolding. Since, as Luxemburg recognised, these consequences are incalculable in their global reach and complexity, the need for international outreach is all-important: not 'internationality' as an overarching abstraction, but 'internationality' as a recognition of the global diversity of local circumstance. Any mode of revolutionary organisation would – and will – have to be responsive to the inconsequentiality of revolutionary action. Without some such recognition, it collapses back into a form of centralised control and command leadership against which the original action – 'the deed' – was in direct and uncompromising opposition.

It was Luxemburg's insistence on the inclusivity of revolutionary action that was a scandal to the various political alignments whose border crossings she regularly traversed. She criticised Bolshevism on the grounds of its over-centralising tendencies and she arraigned the SPD on the grounds of its reformism and – as she saw it – its pusil-lanimous response to the First World War. Her legacy was distorted and traduced not only by the Stalinist regime but also by the USSR until its historic collapse, and, of course, the Nazi's simply burned her books as a symbol of her supposed irrelevance. But her words survived the flames. What she came to say lives on in the accounts of her life and in her own words: we live and die together in the hope of building together a better world.

Underlying the political urgency of revolutionary action resides an ethical impulse. It rarely declares itself as such, but nevertheless inspires individuals working collectively to acts of intellectual and physical courage, acts of self-sacrifice, and to lives characterised by perseverance, 'grit' and determination. These were the dispositions – the revolutionary virtues or dispositions – that Luxemburg recognised and acknowledged in both herself and in her collaborators. Politics is the constant and nagging reminder that the search for 'the good' – in both our own lives and the lives of others – is undertaken in the rough ground of ethical choice: what kind of a person do I want to be? To what kind of a future do I want my life to have contributed? It is only within the political sphere that these ethical questions – concerning how I conceive of myself in relation to 'goodness' – can relate to the moral questions regarding how I translate that conception of self into my treatment of others.

These ethical questions lie at the heart of Luxemburg's political internationalism. For her, internationalism was grounded in the particular circumstances of people caught up in the exploitation of global capitalism as it impinged on actual lives and communities. Internationalism was not an airy abstraction, but a way of drawing attention to the specificity of suffering at precise points and within specific sectors and across the global outreach of capitalist exploitation and colonial violence. The crucial dividing lines, Luxemburg insisted, were not between nations, but between those for whom capitalism is a means of exploitation and those who bear the brunt of that exploitation. What Luxemburg inveighed against was the fact that human suffering was not an unfortunate and unintended consequence of global capitalism, but an essential element within the logic of capital accumulation.

To be purposeful, one has to look forward – teleologically – to an unpredictable and unforeseeable future, while looking sideways – globally – to the implications of that unpredictable and unforeseeable future for other places and other peoples. One has to dwell in uncertainty: an uncertainty that Luxemburg embraced with what she saw as a necessary cheerfulness. If courage was one of the virtuous dispositions necessary for maintaining the forward momentum, then the encouragement of others was a necessary disposition in building a strong platform of agreement across boundaries. In moving forward, Luxemburg was always reaching out: eyes ahead, arms outstretched.

FUTURE IMAGINARIES

We live in an increasingly differentiated society: differentiated, that is, in terms of its economic, social and civic functioning. In that respect, it is a very different society from the one within which the early socialists of the nineteenth century had developed their thinking. As Honneth puts it, none of the early socialists were willing to recognize the gradual functional differentiation of modern societies. Trapped entirely within the spirit of industrialism, and thus convinced that a future socialist society would be determined exclusively by the sphere of industrial production, they saw no reason to consider the existent or desirable independence of social spheres of action.

(Honneth 2017: 88)

In particular, argues Honneth, 'they saw no reason to develop an independent semantics of freedom for the sphere of love, marriage and the family' (2017: 85) or for 'the sphere of democratic politics' (2017: 89). The economy was the single, central authority in the functioning of society, which was conceived of as 'an order steered centrally from below, i.e. from within the relations of production' (2017: 93).

Luxemburg never developed a sociological analysis based on the functional differentiation of society as proposed by Honneth. Nevertheless, she does anticipate a more expansive notion of freedom that Honneth is here advocating: a notion of freedom that encompasses the interpersonal and civic as well as the economic. Economic freedom alone cannot guarantee freedom and equality within, for example, the institutions of marriage and civil partnership or the institutions and organisations that represent us within the public sphere. Patriarchy is not confined to the economically impoverished. On the contrary, it is alive and kicking among those whose economic freedom remains largely unaccountable and unregulated. Nor can economic freedom alone secure democratic rights, which are routinely trampled over in the interests of international corporations, global trade and private greed.

This assortment of iniquities and inequalities is now invariably bundled into the category termed 'neoliberalism': an ideology that has clearly lost much of its credibility but nevertheless continues to exert influence not least – as Marnie Holborow (2015) has shown – through its permeation of everyday language use and organisational cultures. Luxemburg did not have this particular category to hand, but she understood that the ideological workings of capitalism were complex and far-reaching; that their tentacular roots reach down

POLITICAL PURPOSE · 117

into the interpersonal and the private; that they permeate our public institutions and organisational structures of society. She intuited a totality of social practices that could not be accommodated by the notion of an economic base supporting a cultural and social super-structure. She showed in her life and work how the struggle for economic, social and civic freedom could only come together in all its complicated strivings within a whole way of life.

Love and friendship – *eros* and *philia* – were central to her life's work. Her close personal relationships with men and women sustained and supported her and provided her with a sense of what she termed 'the socialization of society': society not as an abstraction but as a lived and living reality. She was a feminist for whom 'the proletarian woman' was the major protagonist in a gender-inclusive struggle for women's rights. She was an uncompromising individ-ualist, who – while rejecting the ideology of liberal individualism – nevertheless insisted on the right of individuals to think differently and to live their lives accordingly. In an essay on Tolstoy published in 1908, she acknowledged that he 'has the least understanding of Social Democracy and the modern labour movement', but insisted on his importance as a free and independent thinker: 'he has to go his own way with every thought' (RPL: 21–22). The freedom to think differently within the public sphere and to be oneself within the personal and interpersonal sphere of action was crucial to what Luxemburg understood by democratic socialism.

Democratic ways of working formed the bedrock of Luxemburg's socialism. She developed her skills as a writer and editor within what we would now term fringe journalism and worked her way through to one of the major political commentators of her day, working across the spectrum of journalistic and publishing outlets. At the same time, she was active as an electioneer and as a public speaker and polemicist. She refused to accept what she saw as a false dichotomy between reformism and revolution, believing that both parliamen-tary and extra-parliamentary means were necessary in the struggle to democratic socialism. Even as late as the founding conference of the KPD, in late December 1918, she was arguing the case for the KPD to be represented in the newly formed National Assembly (R: 369).

During her years in Zurich as a student and in her early years in Germany, Luxemburg experienced the consequences of economic dependency and understood at first hand its impact on personal relationships. She was far from naive regarding the effects of economic disadvantage on herself and others. She understood the brute force of poverty. But she also understood how freedom has to be achieved on many fronts: through interpersonal relationships and civic participation and engagement as well as through the struggle against economic inequality. For Luxemburg, these were not subsystems of some larger systemic whole, but were unified in how she went about her life as a deeply humanistic, democratic socialist.

In her 1913 assessment of Ferdinand Lascelles – active in the revolutionary period of the late 1840s, a key figure in the formation of the SPD in 1875, but seen as something of a maverick within Marxist circles – Luxemburg emphasised that '[t]he time of towering individuals, of leaders rushing boldly ahead, is past' (RPL: 28), but nevertheless acknowledged the supreme importance of the political programme that Lascelles had helped to advance:

> Social Democracy ... is the powerful driving wheel of social progress in the Empire; it is the refuge of scholarly research and art; it is the only attorney for the equal rights of the female sex; it is the protector and awakener of the popular youth; it is the bulwark of international peace, the resurrection of millions from the deep pit of material and spiritual misery to which capitalist exploitation has banished them.
>
> (RPL: 28)

Freedom – in what is an increasingly complex and differentiated world – is never one single and uncomplicated thing. It is, as Luxemburg maintained, 'the refuge of scholarly research and art', 'the only attorney for the equal rights of the female sex', 'the protector and awakener of the popular youth', 'the bulwark of international peace', and 'the resurrection of millions from the deep pit of material and spiritual misery to which capitalist exploitation has banished them' (RPL: 28).

Luxemburg was looking back over a 50-year period of socialist struggle, but her words resonate in what was her future and our present: a present in which freedom has to be pursued on many fronts and by many diverse routes and passages, but, always, as Honneth puts it, 'as an organic whole of independent and yet purposefully cooperating functions in which the members act for each other in social freedom.' The politics resides in that crucial phrase, 'the members act for each other', which raises vital questions as to what constitutes membership and belongingness in an increasingly fragmented and unequal world and what 'act[ing] for each other' might mean in the very dangerous world of demagogy and post-truth politics that we now inhabit (1917: 93).

* * *

The following two chapters shift from a broad discussion of Luxemburg's ideas – the significance of the social in the political struggle, the importance of critical consciousness in the formation of the political agent, and the primacy of action in defining political purpose – to some reflections on the traces she has left behind. Where might we look for those traces? How would we recognise them, if we saw them? Where might they lead us? These questions become particularly pressing at a time when democracy risks tipping over into the kind of populist authoritarianism that in Europe characterised the decades immediately following Luxemburg's murder. To discover the traces – and address the questions – is to find possible ways forward.

PART III

Thinking Differently

Freedom is always and exclusively freedom for the one who thinks differently.

Rosa Luxemburg, 1918, *The Russian Revolution* (R: 305)

6

History is Now

'THE ANGEL OF HISTORY'

Luxemburg is a pivotal figure in the history of Marxism. Her insistence on the fundamental importance of the economy echoes the preoccupations of the early socialists of the nineteenth century, while her emphasis on the 'socialization of society' anticipate many of the preoccupations of the radical left in the twentieth century. Similarly, while her appeal to 'the proletariat' evokes the industrial landscape of that earlier century, her focus on the prime importance of consciousness speaks more directly to our post-industrial times. And, although an element of historical determinism is implicit in her belief in the final and inevitable collapse of capitalism, her radical uncertainty regarding the consequences of that collapse suggest a reinterpretation of some of the basic tenets of Marxism.

But while it is possible to view Luxemburg as a 'forerunner' of later movements, trends and intellectual developments, it is also important to bear in mind that she had no sense of herself as a 'transitional' figure. Whatever grand narrative we may retrospectively locate her within is of our making. She – like us – can only stand in the present moment facing the storm of consequentiality blowing in from the past. Benjamin characterised this existential human figure as 'the angel of history'. In the ninth of his 'Theses on the Philosophy of History', he reflects on a painting named 'Angelus Novus' by the Swiss-German artist Paul Klee:

His eyes are staring, his mouth is open, his wings are spread. This is how one pictures the angel of history. His face is turned toward the past. Where we perceive a chain of events, he sees one single catastrophe which keeps piling wreckage upon wreckage and hurls it in front of his feet. The angel would like to stay, awaken the dead, and make whole what has been smashed. But a storm is blowing from Paradise, it has got caught in his wings with such violence that the angel can no longer close them. This storm irresistibly propels him into the future to which his back is turned, while the pile of debris before him grows skyward. This storm is what we call progress.

(Benjamin [1968] 2007: 257–258)

Benjamin – writing at the outset of the Second World War – evokes this image of 'the angel of history' in order to counter the rhetoric of human progress, by means of which totalitarian regimes seek to justify the violence they commit on the grounds of historical necessity. Totalitarian ideologies would only be defeated, he argued, when the underlying conception of history from which they derived their legitimacy was refuted. The face of 'the angel of history' is turned toward the past in order to fully recall and do justice to the suffering of the past. What we call 'progress' is – to pursue Benjamin's metaphor – the storm of consequence stirred up by past deeds and forever breaking upon the present.

To view Luxemburg as 'the angel of history' is to remind ourselves that – although in retrospect she can be seen as a 'forerunner' or 'transitional' figure, she lived in the present: a present that she sought to understand by questioning the received record of the past. She spent her life committed to what Benjamin defined as the prime task of historical materialism: 'to brush history against the grain' ([1968] 2007: 257). If the grain of received historical narrative is one of distortion and forgetfulness, then the prime task is to use all the available resources of critique and remembrance to brush against it. Luxemburg did precisely that in exposing the circle of human suffering that led, for example, from the cotton mills of Lancashire, through the slave plantations of the southern states, to the rice beds of Orissa. Here was no grand narrative of capitalist progression, but a tawdry story of imperialist incompetence and the ruthless drive towards power and possession.

In the women's prison in Barnimstrasse, Berlin, Luxemburg also recorded in *The Junius Pamphlet* the human suffering and loss inflicted by the First World War. 'Never has a war killed off whole nations; never, within the past century, has it swept over all of the great and established lands of civilized Europe.' In the peroration of this great anti-war pamphlet and condemnation of the First World War, Luxemburg recorded the loss of life and human carnage in:

> the Vosges, in the Ardennes, in Belgium, in Poland, in the Carpathians and on the Save; ... [among] the workers of England, France, Belgium, Germany and Russia ... The fruit of the sacrifices and toil of generations is destroyed in a few short weeks.
>
> (R: 339–340)

This was impassioned rhetoric aimed at the false rhetoric of those who sought to aggrandise war; it was real history posed against the distorted and forgetful history of the would-be victors; it was truth composed in a prison cell and spoken to power.

What we now know – but only in part – is what Luxemburg could not know: the suffering that followed the suffering; the pile of debris that, as Benjamin put it, grows skyward; the irreversible consequences of the war to end all wars (all wars are waged on that banal premise). For, as Gerwarth has argued, the way in which the First World War ended was as tragic in its consequences as the way in which it was conducted. The thesis he advances is:

> that in order to understand the violent trajectories that Europe – including Russia and the former ottoman lands in the Middle East – followed throughout the twentieth century, we must look not so much at war experiences between 1914 and 1917 as at the way in which the war ended for the vanquished states of the Great War: in defeat, imperial collapse and revolutionary turmoil.
>
> (Gerwarth 2017: 13)

What resulted from this period of 'defeat, imperial collapse and revolutionary turmoil' were two totalitarian regimes – Nazism and Stalinism – that wrought havoc and human devastation on a global and unprecedented scale. The neoliberal order that followed – characterised by Wolin (2010) as 'the specter of inverted totalitarianism' – was premised on an exponential rise in global and domestic levels of economic inequality (invariably justified, of course, as a necessary corollary of economic progress). The sustainability of that neoliberal order has, since the global financial crisis of 2007, been the subject of continuing debate – as has the nature of whatever economic order may follow (see, for example, Crouch 2011; Mason 2015; Streeck 2016, 2017). The future is as uncertain in our own day as it was for Luxemburg 100 years ago.

But there is a great deal of history between Luxemburg and ourselves, and we cannot simply leapfrog over it. We have to find a common space in which Luxemburg is present not as judge or prophet, arbiter or seer, but as a questioner: someone with whom we are able to meet half way and understand the questions she might be asking of us in our present circumstances. The philosopher Hans-Georg Gadamer describes this in-between space as 'the fusion of horizons'. As I move towards or away from the object of perception, its horizon shifts as I encounter it from different temporal and spatial locations: hence, 'the fundamental non-definitiveness of the horizon in which [our] understanding moves' (Gadamer 2004: 366). Or, as Joseph Dunne puts it, 'the interpreter's horizon is already being stretched beyond itself, so that it is no longer the same horizon that it was independently of this encounter' (1997: 121). Because both interpreter and interpreted are located in the process of history, the horizon of interpretation can never achieve permanent fixity. Each interpretation is, therefore, both unique and open to reinterpretation: 'horizons are not rigid but mobile' (Gadamer 2001: 48).

The struggle *against* global exploitation and *for* democratic socialism – a struggle that Luxemburg helped define and was instrumental in carrying forward – continues on many fronts. But just as Luxemburg had to reinterpret that struggle for her own time and place, so we have to rethink it for our own particular circumstances. This rethinking constitutes an interruption – a moment of discontinuity – in which we seek to identify and address the questions that Luxemburg might be asking of us: not the easy solutions that we might derive from her legacy, but the hard questions that she continues to pose. We identify these questions through, on the one hand, sustained attentiveness to the details of Luxemburg's life, work and context, and, on the other hand, a critical awareness of the context within which we are ourselves located. Only when the attentiveness and the awareness fuse is it possible to give the past a new life in the present – or, to draw on Said's fine phrase, to locate it within 'widening circles of pertinence' (2004: 80).

THE STRUGGLE FOR DEMOCRACY

In his 2006 *The Culture of the New Capitalism*, the sociologist Richard Sennett set himself the task of searching for the 'ideal man or woman' that would be compatible with 'the new capitalism'. He did so by pulling together the extensive research that he had conducted on the changing labour market during the preceding years. Much of that research was based on interview evidence with workers in a variety of industries and public services (see, for example, Sennett: 1999). He argued that the 'ideal man or woman' would have to be adaptable to an unstable and fragmentary society characterised by short-term relationships 'while migrating from task to task, job to job, place to place'; have to be able to survive in a working environment in which 'the shelf life of many skills is short'; and be able 'to let go of the past' when head of companies can routinely assert 'that past service in particular earns no employee a guaranteed place' (Sennett 2006: 4).

The 'institutional architecture' within which this 'ideal man or woman' would have to operate was characterised by 'the delayering of institutions' (whereby organisations shed organisational layers through the out-sourcing of some functions to other firms or other places); the 'casualisation' of the labour force (short-term contracts allow employers to avoid paying benefits and to move workers from task to task with contracts altered to suit the changing priorities of the firm); and 'non-linear sequencing' (immediate and small tasks become the emphasis within an overall shortening of the organisation's time frame) (Sennett 2006: 48–49). These organisational factors, argued Sennett led to 'lower institutional loyalties, diminishment of informal trust among workers, and weakening of institutional knowledge' (Sennett 2006: 63). This, in turn leads to a 'new geography of power, the center controlling the peripheries of power in institutions with ever fewer intermediate layers of bureaucracy' (Sennett 2006: 81).

The irony that Sennett highlights is that 'the ideal man or woman' is a hugely diminished human being. Far from being empowered by 'the new capitalism', he or she is haunted by 'the specter of uselessness' (Sennett 2006: 86) and devoid of 'a sense of *narrative movement*' (Sennett 2006: 183, emphasis in original). The ideal functionaries of the capitalist order are thus perfectly attuned to chronic social fragmentation and instability and accepting of – or in denial of – the deleterious effects of that fragmentation and instability on their own lives and the lives of others. Moreover, this 'ideal' of manhood and womanhood applies not to any particular group or class, but operates as a homogenising norm to which all are expected to aspire. The culture of 'the new capitalism' thereby becomes the totalising ideology of a deeply fragmented and unstable society.

Sennett is focusing primarily on the implications of 'the new capitalism' for the West. However, those implications are evident much farther afield: in, for example, the exploitation by corporate business of developing countries and their natural resources; the crippling and chronic indebtedness incurred by those countries and the conditions imposed upon their governments in respect of repayment; the destruction of traditional ways of working and living together and the consequent displacement of families and whole communities. Luxemburg's insistence on capitalism's relentless drive towards global exploitation – and the devastating effect of that exploitation on workers and on those whose resources are plundered in the name of progress – finds its apotheosis in the workings of twenty-first century capitalism.

So how within this globally fragmented context can new and inclusive solidarities be forged in response to specific circumstances? How can these solidarities respond creatively to the need for forms of resistance that are alert to the particularities of those circumstances? How can broader coalitions of resistance and mutual support be formed so as to ensure the sustainability of the struggle-not-yet-finished?

Collective struggle

Ahdaf Soueif provides us with a first-hand account of how, under exceptional circumstances, collective action remains a possibility. Her diary account of the days preceding the toppling of Hosni Mubarak on 11 February 2011 was written as events in Egypt unfolded. We read her account against our retrospective understanding of the outcomes of the events she is describing, but for her those outcomes were unknowable: 'you, as you read,' she reminds her readers, 'know a great deal more than I can know' (2012: 186). In retrospect, the events chronicled by Soueif can be interpreted as tragic given the situation currently pertaining in Egypt and across much of the Arab world. But Soueif is concerned primarily with what those events meant at the time for those involved:

> I believe that optimism is a duty; if people had not been optimistic on 25 January, and all the days that followed, they would not have left their homes or put their wonderful, strong, vulnerable human bodies on the streets. Our revolution would not have happened.
>
> (Soueif 2012: 186)

Soueif's account places her own – and her fellow citizens' – love of Cairo at the heart of her story: 'a story about me and my city; the city I so love and have so sorrowed for these twenty years and more ... [H]er memories are our memories, her fate is our fate' (2012: 8–9). For Soueif – as for many of her fellow Cairenes – the imminent sale of the public spaces at the centre of Cairo was the crucial catalyst for revolutionary action:

> we found out that the regime had been planning to sell Tahrir. They'd been planning to sell the central public space in our capital to a hotel chain, to a foreign hotel chain ... [W]e knew that everything was up for sale: land monuments, islands, lakes, beaches, people's homes, antiquities, stretches of the Nile, natural resources, people, sovereignty, national parks, human organs, goldmines, the wealth under the ground, the water in the river, the labour of the people – everything.
>
> (Soueif 2012: 113)

Midan el-Tahrir – or Tahrir Square – is the central point of Greater Cairo and is not so much a square or circle as a massive curved rectangle covering about 45,000 square metres. Soueif tells us that she prefers to describe the area using the Arabic word, '*midan*', because 'it does not tie you down to a shape but describes an open urban space in a central position in a city' (2012: 10). The Midan has not only geographical significance located as it is at the heart of Cairo, but also emotional and political resonance as the historic meeting place and forum of the city. It was natural, therefore, that when the people of Cairo took to the streets on 28 January they should have gathered in Midan el-Tahrir, since it was 'home to the civic spirit' (2012: 11). It was natural, also, that, when the people's delegations came to the Midan from other cities and the provinces to set up their banners, they should join together in chanting: 'legitimacy comes from Tahrir' (2012: 14).

The Midan provided a public space in which the collective action of the citizenry could present itself to the world. Paradoxically, as one of the young revolutionaries quoted by Soueif pointed out, it was because Tahrir was pure spectacle that it became an undeniable reality as people around the world watched events unfold on their television screens and via YouTube:

> The people know that Tahrir was simply spectacle. They know that the revolution was won in the streets and the factories. But they also know that the spectacle is important in the battle of ideas, and if Tahrir falls, the dream falls. Tahrir is a myth that creates a reality in which we've long believed.
>
> (Soueif 2012: 190)

Three words in particular point to what was – and remains – distinctive about that 'myth'. The first word is '*selmeyya*'. Meaning 'peaceful', '*selmeyya*' is the Arabic word that was constantly chanted by the demonstrators as they faced the combined violence of cavalry, Molotovs, snipers and militias. It was not, insists Soueif, fear of violence that held the demonstrators back: 'No, we the people were implementing a doctrine of minimum force, minimum destruction. This was a revolution that respected the law, that had at its heart the desire to reclaim the institutions of the state, not to destroy them' (2012: 168). She provides a vivid illustration of that doctrine in action. One of her friends, who had remained off the streets during the violence, decided she would venture out. A young man volunteered to accompany her to her car:

On the steps he told her he was a butcher and had looked at his knives that morning and considered. 'But then,' he said, 'I reckoned we really wanted to keep it selmeyya so I didn't bring any.' He held her arm to run to her car and as they ran he was taken. 'I tried to hold him,' she says, 'but they took him … He was on the ground and five men were kicking him.' Every few metres, she said, there would be a group gathered around a fallen young man kicking his head in.
(Soueif 2012: 139–140)

The second word is 'shabab' which derives from the root 'sh/b' to grow. Soueif tells us that:

it carries the same emotional load as 'youth' with an extra dash of vigour … Unpacked it carries the signification of 'people, men and women, who are at the youthful stage of life with all its energy, hope, optimism, vigour, impulsiveness and love of life, and who are acting communally, together.'
(Soueif 2012: 196)

The shabab led the revolution. They were central to its spontaneity, organisation, discipline and persistence. When they were not holding the front line, maintaining the flow of information and provisions, rushing the injured to makeshift field hospitals, they kept up an insistent drumming:

A loud, energetic, rhythmic drumming, drumming, drumming on the metal shield … They keep it up all night long. It tells any approaching regime baltagi that the shabab are awake and waiting and it helps to keep everybody going; it says we're here, we're here, we're undefeated.
(Soueif 2012: 139)

It was the shabab – the young people of Egypt some of whom were not old enough to vote in the elections held the following year – who made the 'Arab Spring' possible, 'because it was they who changed the world, and it now belongs to them' (Soueif 2012: 187).

Many of those young people died in and around the Midan and elsewhere in Egypt. The third word – '*shuhada*' – defines those who died as martyrs. The point about defining a particular death as martyrdom is to highlight its enduring symbolic value. The life of the martyr gains meaning from its afterlife. For the *shuhada*, as evoked in Soueif's account, that afterlife is *now*: not another world, but this world; not eternal, but temporal; not abstracted from history, but integral to it. The *shuhada* help the living to define their ends and purposes in this world and in the here and now. That, Soueif seems to suggest, is their supreme legacy.

As the people of Egypt gathered in Tahrir Square on the evening of Friday 11 February, after Mubarak had stepped aside and the armed forces were in control of Egypt, Soueif wrote in her diary:

> And in the centre of the Midan a stillness. The pictures of the murdered. The shuhada. Sally Zahran, massive blows to the head, glances upwards and smiles. Muhammad Abd el-Menem, shot in the head, his hair carefully gelled. Ali Muhsin, shot, carries a laughing toddler with a big blue sea behind him. Muhammad Bassiouny, shot, lies back with his two kids ... Ihab Muhammadi smiles but his eyes are thoughtful ... and more, 843 more. In the triumph and joy and uncertainty of the moment, they are the still centre ... Our future has been paid for with their lives.'
>
> (Soueif 2012: 181)

The words '*selmeyya*', '*shabab*' and '*shuhada*' convey something of the collective experience that brought people together and which relied upon – while at the same time generating – immensely strong bonds of friendship. Survival was dependent on existing friendships and on friendships formed swiftly and sometimes pragmatically in life-threatening situations. It was also dependent on a collective bond of trust between those who had chosen to take the immense risk of being present in the Midan:

once you're inside, the Midan is amazing … Everyone is suddenly, miraculously, completely themselves. Everyone understands. We're all very gentle with each other … Our selves are in our hands, precious, newly recovered, perhaps fragile; we know we must be careful of our own and of each other's.

(Soueif 2012: 159)

The organisation of collective action, which included uprisings not only in Cairo but also across the major cities of Egypt – in Alexandria, Suez, Port Said, Beni Sweif, Mansoura and el-Mahalla – sprang from and formed around the mutual trust that characterised the early days of the Spring 2011 revolution. 'It was,' as M. Cherif Bassiouni puts it, 'magnificently naïve – an extraordinary, patriotic, and nationalistic movement involving many segments of society' (2016: 58). But it was also deeply creative in the interplay of collective action and spontaneous organisation.

Creative struggle

That interplay is one of the major themes of Ness's (2016) analysis of new forms of worker organisation in China, India and South Africa. Foreign investment coupled with neoliberal economic policies – supported by the World Bank and the International Monetary Fund – has constituted a new wave of capitalist imperialism that relies heavily on internal and external migration. It is the impact of this new wave of expansionism – and the creativity with which workers are responding to it – that is the subject of Ness's analysis.

The existing organisational structures created to maintain workers' rights have, argues Ness, proved inadequate within this new context of Third World capitalist imperialism. Workers are, therefore, thinking outside those structures in order to develop new forms of association and solidarity:

a profound movement is emerging among workers demanding action on grievances outside the system of established unions. Workers' movements are operating within the interstices of existing trade union structures, with or without the sanction of the unions.

Rank-and-file workers in industries are forming independent associations and compelling existing unions to represent their interests.

(Ness 2016: 189)

He shows that in India 'workers are forming independent unions to represent their interests'; in China 'rank-and-file committees have been effective in advancing worker interests when local unions fail to represent their members'; and in South Africa '[w]orker self-organizing expanded across South Africa's mining sector from 2009 to 2014, culminating in a five-month nationwide strike of platinum miners against mining conglomerates' (Ness 2016: 189–190).

Within South Africa, the powerful Tripartite Alliance – formed as the apartheid system was collapsing and comprising the African National Congress, the South African Communist Party and the Congress of South African Trade Unions – was no longer seen by some of the most vulnerable workers as representing their particular interests. The platinum miners' action taken in defiance of the combined might of the National Union of Miners and the Congress of South African Trade Unions illustrates both the inadequacy of these existing organisations in protecting the rights and interest of workers and the capacity of the workers to create new post-apartheid solidarities and structures of resistance.

On 12 January 2012, Impala Platinum Holdings Limited (Implats), one of South Africa's three largest platinum-mining firms, announced an 18 per cent monthly wage increase for local workers employed at its largest facility located in Rustenburg. However, the rock drill operators – chiefly migrant labourers recruited from rural regions in the Eastern Cape and Lesotho and working under the most dangerous conditions – were excluded from this agreement that had been brokered by the National Union of Mineworkers, which was affiliated to the Congress of South African Trade Unions. In defiance of the union, they proceeded to withdraw their labour. On 24 January, Implats responded by terminating their contracts and stipulating that they return to work by 27 January as new hires, thereby losing their accrued pension benefits. On 30 January, the strike spread to the majority of all workers at Implats in support of the dismissed rock drill operators. In February, the National Union of Mineworkers and the Congress of South African Trade Unions declared the strike illegal and called on Implats to reinstate the workers without the previously announced 18 per cent wage increase. However, in April, Implats – under increased pressure from the workers – agreed to restore the wage increase, and following further negotiations, agreed a wage increase for the rock drill operators.

The crucial point in this case – which is only one of many that Ness documents – is that a disparate group of vulnerable workers from different regions and cultures were able to forge new bonds of solidarity in spite of there being no pre-existing organisational structure that could adequately support them. 'For the duration of the strike,' writes Ness, 'the rank and file workers formed assemblies that held regular meetings and collectively deliberated a tactical strategy that challenged the National Union of Mineworkers' resolutions imposed by its central bureaucracy'. The rock drillers – working underground in the mines and at the hard end of danger – acted on the basis of their own unsanctioned and unauthorised political agency. Moreover, when subject to victimisation by their employer, they were supported by the majority of their co-workers. As Ness points out, their collective action demonstrates how 'organizational representation is subordinate to the workers' movements themselves' (2016: 190).

It also demonstrates that the creativity of struggle lies in its grasp of the social totality. The presenting issue for the rock drillers and their co-workers who joined them in collective action was one of economic injustice: a wage increase had been denied to a group of workers who were at once highly vulnerable because of their migrant status and who also operated at the sharp edge of risk within the workplace. But the underlying issues included the demand by the rock drillers for recognition of their equal rights as workers and their equal worth as human beings. The power lay in collective action, but that collective action was only possible because the workforce as a whole were conscious of the injustice of the rock drillers' situation – and that of their families and dependents – and were committed to challenging that injustice.

The struggle for political justice is always creative, experimental and unpredictable, because it necessarily involves new understandings, new solidarities and new associative frameworks. The platinum miners' insurgency involved the questioning of old assumptions and the raising of consciousness regarding the plight of a particular group of workers and their families and dependents. It also involved the breaking of old and traditional solidarities based on the authority of the immensely powerful and influential Tripartite Alliance together with the forging of new solidarities among workers from diverse cultural, national and regional backgrounds. Finally, it involved the development of new organisational frameworks in the form of the worker's assemblies and their regular meetings and collective deliberations.

Struggle-not-yet-finished

Luxemburg understood that there is a crucial distinction between possessing rights and being able to exercise them. Constitutions, parliaments and states can confer rights, but, unless they provide the conditions necessary for those on whom the rights are conferred to exercise those rights, the possession of rights is largely meaningless. She also understood that it is much easier to pass on to future generations the legal or constitutional possession of rights than to establish the conditions necessary for their fulfilment. The possession of rights that is in itself the result of immense and prolonged struggle does not – and cannot – ensure closure. The longer and harder struggle is to ensure the conditions necessary for each new generation to exercise those rights. That is always the struggle-not-yet-finished: a struggle that requires its own cross-generational momentum and its own structures of cultural and associative transmission.

Martha C. Nussbaum (2000), writing with reference to the experience of women living in the rural areas of Andhra Pradesh in southern India, makes precisely this point:

> All women in India have equal rights under the Constitution; but in the absence of effective enforcement of laws against rape and Supreme Court guidelines on sexual harassment, economic

empowerment, and in the absence of programs targeted at increasing female literacy, economic empowerment, and employment opportunities, those rights are not real to them ... In short, liberty is not just a matter of having rights on paper, it requires being in a position to exercise those rights.

(Nussbaum 2000: 54)

Nussbaum's study of women's collectives in rural India provides important insights into how fragile and provisional structures of cooperation and mutual support can coalesce around an awareness of shared injustice and a shared commitment to countering that injustice.

In the course of the study – conducted between March 1997 and December 1998 – Nussbaum found that domestic violence was one of the first issues women typically wished to discuss: 'When the Andhra Pradesh women (all illiterate) made drawings of their problems, wife-beating and child sexual abuse were both absolutely central' (2000: 294). She also found that the collectives provided them with an opportunity to share their thoughts and experiences. This sharing involved what she calls 'a two-stage process of awareness: coming to see themselves as in a bad situation, and coming to see themselves as citizens who had a right to a better situation' (2000: 140). For most of the women concerned, achieving 'a better situation' involved gaining some measure of economic self-sufficiency, since this would strengthen 'the bargaining position' of the women by increasing their options, changing the way in which they were perceived within the family and community, and providing them with a sense of self-worth. (2000: 283–290)

At this point, the local grass-roots collectives were able to link into a broader-based organisation of poor, self-employed women workers: the Self-Employed Women's Association (SEWA), which was registered in 1972 as a trade union of women who earn a living through their own labour or small businesses. These women, unlike those employed in the organised sector, do not obtain regular salaried employment with welfare benefits (of the female labour force in India, more than 94 per cent are in the unorganised sector). SEWA – the organisation – has spawned a broader movement which, as Nussbaum suggests, 'translated the Gandhian idea of India's self-sufficiency in the colonial struggle against Britain onto the plane of the family and the village, where women, too, struggle to be free from a quasi-colonial oppression' (2000: 67; for the history and development of the SEWA movement, see Rose 1993).

One of the mechanisms SEWA uses to translate this idea into practice is the SEWA Cooperative Bank. Established in 1974, the bank is owned by the self-employed women as shareholders. They fund the bank through their savings and set the loan rates. The bank offers very small loans (or 'microcredits') to borrowers who typically lack collateral, steady employment or credit history and who would therefore be unable to gain financial assistance from mainstream banks and would be at risk from loan sharks or corrupt banks offering exorbitant interest rates. As Amola and Shahir Bhatt have shown in their recent evaluative study, the bank has proved remarkably successful in 'empowering the members by providing them with financial resources and assistance and support' (2016: 57).

Nussbaum cites as an example of the significance of SEWA in transforming women's lives the case of Vasanti, a young woman in her early 30s who, having managed to divorce her abusive husband, had moved from one state of economic dependency to another. She was no longer dependent on an abusive husband, but was still reliant on her brothers, who although supportive had their own families to support. 'Vasanti', as Nussbaum puts it, 'thus remained highly vulnerable and lacking in confidence' (2000: 106). A loan from SEWA changed this picture. She now had independent control over her livelihood. She owed a lot of money, but she owed it to a mutually supportive community of women. Dependency had been replaced by mutuality. Reflecting on the transformation in Vasanti, Nussbaum writes:

By now, Vasanti is animated; she is looking us straight in the eye, and her voice is strong and clear. Women in India have a lot of pain, she says. And I, I have quite a lot of sorrow in my life. But from the pain, our strength is born. Now that we are doing better ourselves, we want to do some good for other women, to feel that we are good human beings.

(Nussbaum 2000: 17)

Nussbaum concludes her study by quoting from an annual report, which included a collective record of the Andhra Pradesh women's plans for the future. Among those plans was a statement of the women's aspirations. Here are a few of them: 'We want to plant fruit trees in front of our houses ...', 'We will build our houses ourselves ...', 'We want our school to run better ...', 'We want more women to join us ...', 'Our children ... should learn new things' (2000: 302).

The struggle for the women of Andhra Pradesh is not-yet-finished because each succeeding generation has not only to fight for its rights, but also to fight for the conditions necessary to exercise those rights within the ever-changing circumstances in which they find themselves. It is also a struggle-not-yet-finished because – as in this case – economic and social factors are deeply entwined, and understanding the one while resolving the other takes time. Sexual domination cannot be explained wholly in terms of economic dependency. Nor can economic independence alone entirely eradicate it. Multiple factors are in play. Nevertheless, Nussbaum's general point holds true: 'various liberties of choice have material preconditions, in whose absence there is merely a simulacrum of choice' (2000: 53).

The sustainability of the struggle is made possible because SEWA – as both an organisation and as a movement – provides a social and economic space within which the individual and collective concerns of succeeding generations of women can be acknowledged and where they have access to broader coalitions of resistance and wider networks of mutual support. As such, it constitutes a decentralised network of mutual 'service' (SEWA means 'service' in several Indian languages) for sharing resources and ensuring the sustainability of local initiatives. The empowerment of each is achieved through the collective power of all.

THE OPENNESS OF HISTORY

We cannot determine the outcomes of our individual actions, because the consequences of those actions necessarily collide and our original intentions become caught in a boundless process of action and reaction. But by acting together, we can increase the likelihood of articulating and thereby achieving our common ends and purposes.

That is why authoritarian and totalitarian regimes always seek to destroy or control the associative bonds and organisational structures of civil society. For those who seek to determine the destiny of others, collective action is the ultimate threat and the atomisation of society is the strategic goal. Only by acting together can we maintain the openness of history while shaping it from within.

This was Luxemburg's basic premise: we make history in the context of its boundless unpredictability and openness. It was not – and she would not have claimed it to be – an original insight. For her, that insight was fundamental to the Marxist tradition, which had helped form her thinking – and, of course, Marx in this general insight regarding the nature of history was building on earlier traditions of Aristotelian and Hegelian thinking. Nevertheless, in premising her life and work on the assumption that human beings can collectively shape history – and that capitalism was not the end of history but embedded within history – she generated some important questions that are highly relevant 100 years after her murder: questions regarding the nature of the struggle for democratic renewal and how that struggle can be carried forward.

Soueif provides us with a first-hand account of what collective action meant in Egypt in spring 2011. It meant – among other things – drawing on the common resources of friendship, family, civic and religious affiliations and the kindness of strangers in forging new solidarities and a new sense of collective purpose. It meant inclusivity and mutuality. It may well be the case that, as Adam Roberts writes in his reflections on civil resistance and the 'Arab Spring',

> many people in the pro-democracy movements, as well as many outside them, failed to recognize how complicated and dangerous the process of building a new constitutional order would prove to be, how necessary it was to prepare for it, how different the conditions were in each country, how deep social and religious divisions within societies could be, and how tenaciously some rulers would hang onto power.
>
> (Roberts 2016: 324)

But Luxemburg would, I think, ask us to question this all too easy conclusion. After all, who was in a position to recognise how complicated and dangerous the process would be? Who were these people who could sit back and prepare for some future order and assess the different conditions in each country? How might they have been expected to develop a coordinated response on the basis of their understanding of the deep social and religious divisions across the region? What were they expected to do in the face of the obvious fact that authoritarian rulers will be ruthless in their attempt to hang on to power?

We return to Luxemburg's central insight into the necessary 'prematurity' of all revolutionary action. If the people who collected on the streets of the major cities of Egypt had waited for the right time – for the most propitious circumstances – there would have been no revolution. And if there had been no revolution – albeit, like the German Revolution of 1918–1919, a 'failed' revolution – there would have been no affirmation of the openness of history, of the power of collective action, and of the vulnerability of authoritarian leaders and their regimes in seeking to control history in their own interests regardless of the interests of others. The sheer intelligence of Luxemburg's insight speaks back to the common sense assumptions of those for whom collective action must forever wait on circumstance – and, therefore, be endlessly deferred.

Revolutionary action, as Luxemburg conceived it, is an act of faith, not in the inevitability of a specific outcome, but in the human capacity to cope with and carry forward the unfinished business that such action inevitably brings. As such, it requires creativity in looking for alternative ways forward, new alliances and formations, new openings and opportunities. Luxemburg was adept at using existing structures, but she was also constantly building bridges across those structures and forming new solidarities where the existing ones were inadequate or defunct. That same tenacity and creativity was evident in the South African platinum miners' action of 2012. The rock drillers had to defy the old solidarities – the Tripartite Alliance – and rebuild their collective action through small assembles of workers and by reaching out to the wider workforce.

The problem occurs when solidarities become solidified around already articulated interests. They then run the risk of failing to recognise – or even denying the efficacy of – other interests that have not been articulated at all. As far as the organisations comprising the Tripartite Alliance were concerned – organisations that included two radical left-wing political parties and one which represented trade unions across South Africa – the interests of the rock drillers fell outside their frame of recognition. Luxemburg would probably not have been surprised by this failure of recognition, although she would certainly have been outraged. Dialogue and critical engagement were the lifeblood of democratic socialism as she understood it. Once they are stultified, sidelined or neatly compartmentalised, democratic socialism is put at risk. It is only in the inclusivity and reflexivity of collective action that democratic socialism forms its unique space: a space, which – as the SEWA movement illustrates – is *both* expansive and outward-looking *and* attentive to the local and particular.

All revolutionary events are grounded in the particularity of place and time. But their consequences broaden out across space and across history, as those on the outside of the event – the spectators – begin to grasp its universal significance. The spectators are, as it were, drawn into the action, so that the distinction between insider and outsider – spectator and actor – becomes less clear-cut. '[E]ach genuine revolution,' as Ari-Elmeri Hyvönen puts it, 'is a properly world-political event that radiates rays of inspiration, hope and also concern, throughout the globe' (2014, 92). The broadening and the drawing together are both aspects of the same revolutionary process.

In Luxemburg's 1904 *Organizational Questions of Russian Social Democracy*, she criticised Lenin on the grounds that he was 'concerned principally with the control of party activity and not with its fertilization, *narrowing* and not with *broadening*, with *tying the movement up* and not with *drawing it together*.' Against what she saw as his 'ultra-centralism', she argued that organisation and tactics are not a cause but a consequence of 'a continuing series of great creative acts', which constitute the struggle-not-yet-finished (R: 255–256). Her emphasis on the need for 'fertilization' rather than 'control', 'broadening' rather than 'narrowing', and 'drawing together' rather than 'tying up' is particularly relevant in the century following her murder: a century characterised during its first quarter by deepening social stratification and stigmatisation, extreme economic inequality within and across nations and regions, and the return of the demagogues.

.

7

The Long Revolution

OLIGARCHS TURNED DEMAGOGUES

When particular sections of society bear the brunt of economic decline, population loss and urban decay, a deep sense of unfairness will inevitably result. Moreover, when that sense of unfairness becomes a chronic condition through the failure of successive governments to address the social inequalities resulting from their economic policies, outrage becomes a rational response. Since 'exit' is not an option and one's 'voice' is repeatedly ignored, the only option is what Albert O. Hirschman termed '*voice* as a residual of exit': the residue of one's agency expressed as emphatic and uncompromising acts of rejection (1970: 33–36, emphasis in original). Such acts are driven primarily by the impulse towards negative freedom – *freedom from* constraint – and may have little purchase on the positive freedoms that may then open up: the *freedom to* imagine new political trajectories and build new pathways into the future.

Nevertheless, that impulse can give rise to progressive grass-roots movements that are effective in drawing attention to the gross inequalities within society. Moreover, these movements – even if they do not have a direct impact on policy – may have an indirect impact on the general climate of opinion. But that same impulse may also open the door to individuals, who by claiming to represent the interests of the most vulnerable in society are able to channel popular outrage to their own advantage. Such individuals may be excessively wealthy beyond the wildest dreams of those they claim to represent. They may be inextricably entwined in the global elites against which they vent their rhetorical ire. Indeed, their policies may, after close scrutiny, be seen to privilege those elites. None of these factors would seem to have a bearing on their credibility, which resides solely in their perceived claim to be 'the voice of the people'.

When that credibility achieves legitimacy through the ballot box, we have entered the age of the demagogues: an age in which the rhetoric of populism dominates the political discourse.

'Populism' is a slippery, catch-all term. What does it mean? Jan-Werner Müller (2016) addresses this question by suggesting that it involves two related claims. First, populists claim that 'the voice of the people' takes precedent over all other sources of legitimate political authority: the judiciary, parliament and local government. The complexity of democratic sovereignty is thereby collapsed into a notion of 'the sovereignty of the people' – a notion that licenses populists to decry any attempt by the courts to pursue their constitutional function, to demand that elected members adhere to a popular mandate rather than exercise their independent judgements, and to inveigh against any sections of the free press that are critical of the supposed 'will of the people'. The separation of powers – the constitutional cornerstone of democracy – is thereby put at risk.

Second, populists claim to know what constitutes 'the people'. Within the current political discourse, 'the people' are variously defined as 'ordinary people', 'decent people' and even 'real people'. 'The people', in other words, are invariably defined against 'other people', who by implication are not 'ordinary', not 'decent' and not 'real'. It is these 'other people' who then become the targets – the scapegoats – of populist outrage: immigrants, refugees, religious minorities, recipients of state benefit, the unemployed … the list of potential scapegoats is endless. The point is to define 'the people' against some available 'Other'. Pluralism – the cultural heartbeat of democracy – is thereby not only put at risk but denied.

To those two claims, a third claim should be added. Populists claim a monopoly on the truth regardless of its factual accuracy. The traditional distinction between deception and self-deceptions is not particularly helpful in this context. To tell an untruth with a view to deceiving others is one thing. To tell an untruth that we have wrongly persuaded ourselves is true is another. But to state an untruth that neither seeks to deceive others nor is a consequence of self-deception is something different again. It is an expression of power and control, demanding unconditional assent. It assumes that assent matters more than truth, that to unite around an untruth is justifiable, and that – in the moral wasteland of populism – truth-telling no longer matters. What matters are the so-called 'alternative facts', the rubbishing of serious investigative journalism as 'fake news', and the incessant barrage of half-truths, untruths and downright lies. In the age of the demagogues, post-truth politics reigns supreme.

Lies have always played an important part in maintaining the ideological power base of authoritarian regimes. Writing during the First World War and reflecting from exile on the situation within Europe, Adorno noted in his *Minima Moralia* that:

> the lie has long since lost its honest function of misrepresenting reality. Nobody believes anybody, everyone is in the know. Lies are told only to convey to someone that one has no need either of him or his good opinion.
>
> (Adorno [1951] 2005: 30)

Adorno – having fled Nazi Germany – was writing against the backdrop of the rise of fascism in mid-twentieth-century Europe. But his words continue to have relevance in our own century. Jacques Rancière (2006), writing almost 60 years after the publication of *Minima Moralia*, makes a similar claim regarding the centrality of 'the lie' – the broken promises and culture of mistrust – in the workings of Western representative democracy.

Given that democracy promises to move nearer to 'the power of anyone and everyone', the rules that lay down 'the minimal conditions under which a representative system can be declared democratic' are, Rancière maintains, as follows:

> short and non-renewable electoral mandates that cannot be held concurrently; a monopoly of people's representatives over the formulation of laws; a ban on State functionaries becoming the representatives of the people; a bare minimum of campaigns and campaign costs; and the monitoring of possible interference by economic powers in the electoral process.
>
> (Rancière 2006: 72)

Such rules have nothing extravagant about them. They constitute the bare bones of a promise offered by the elected representatives of democracy to those whom they represent. Yet, as Rancière goes on to argue, that promise – even in its most minimalist form – is rarely kept.

The binding promise – the trust – upon which democracy is founded is routinely broken, and broken in the name of democracy itself:

> eternally elected members holding concurrent or alternating municipal, regional, legislative and/or ministerial functions and whose essential link to the people is that of the representation of regional interests; governments which make laws themselves; representatives of the people that largely come from one adminis-trative school.
>
> (Rancière 2006: 73)

And so Rancière's catalogue of the failures of democracy continues:

> ministers or their collaborators who are also given posts in public or semi-public companies; fraudulent financing of parties through public works contracts; business people who invest colossal sums in trying to win electoral mandates; owners of private media empires that use their public functions to monopolize the empire of the public media. In a word … [t]he evils of which our 'democracies' suffer are primarily evils related to the insatiable appetite of oligarchs. We do not live in democracies.
>
> (Rancière 2006: 73)

Democracy has given legitimacy to the oligarchs and credibility to the demagogues.

What we live in is a mixed form: a form of state founded and legitimised on the privilege of elites and gradually redirected through democratic struggle, but one in which the assumption of elite privilege is layered into the functioning of the state and the workings of society. Rancière argues that:

> The bloody history of struggles for electoral reform in Great Britain is without doubt the best testimony of this, smugly effaced

by the idyllic image of an English tradition of 'liberal' democracy. Universal suffrage is not at all a natural consequence of democracy … [It] is a mixed form, born of oligarchy, redirected by democratic combats and perpetually reconquered by oligarchy.

(Rancière 2006: 54)

A genuine or 'permanent' democracy, he argues elsewhere, can only be guaranteed through 'the continual renewal of the actors and of the forms of their actions, the ever-open possibility of the fresh emergence of this fleeting subject' (Rancière 2007: 61). Here, as elsewhere, Rancière's indictment of 'liberal' democracy and his emphasis on renewal through action echoes Luxemburg's denunciation of 'bourgeois democracy' as enunciated in her 1899 critique of Bernstein and her lifelong insistence on the primacy of political agency.

The oligarchs as ever seek to monopolise power and wealth, but now they do so in the name of 'the people' and with the legitimacy bestowed upon them through the ballot box. This big lie trickles down into a myriad little lies – there is no alternative to economic austerity, inequality is a necessary concomitant of economic growth, immigrants are stealing 'our' jobs, those claiming benefit are 'scroungers' and 'skivers', etc. – whereby the oligarchs turned demagogues create a culture of resentment, nationalism, closure: a false consciousness whereby people lose any sense of what freedoms they are being denied. Luxemburg insisted that the only way to reclaim those freedoms is to understand what freedom is for: to understand what is lost when we are denied the freedom to choose within the economic sphere, the freedom to flourish within the public sphere, and the freedom to become ourselves within the sphere of interpersonal and social relationships.

THE STRUGGLE FOR RENEWAL

But to set about that task of renewal, we must first reject the view of the world of those who claim to speak – and act – on our behalf: a view of the world as constituting the natural order of things, within which there may be some occasional rearrangement of the deckchairs but where the mood music continues to play on. The defenders of that order – those who routinely maintain that there is and can be no alternative – have over the years developed a kind of rhetorical toolkit that they routinely draw on whenever anyone seriously questions that order or suggests radical alternatives.

Hirschman has described that toolkit in some detail. The first item in this toolkit is 'the perversity thesis', according to which any attempt to push society in a certain direction will result in it moving in the opposite direction: 'Attempts to reach for liberty will make society sink into slavery, the quest for democracy will produce oligarchy and tyranny, and social welfare programs will create more, rather than less, poverty. *Everything backfires*' (1991: 12, emphasis in original). When and if 'the perversity thesis' fails to have the desired effect, the defenders of the *status quo* reach for the second item in their rhetorical toolkit: 'the futility thesis', according to which 'the attempt to change is abortive, that in one way or another any alleged change is, was, or will be largely surface, façade, cosmetic, hence illusory, as the "deep" structures of society remain wholly untouched' (Hirschman 1991: 43).

If both the futility and perversity theses fail in their objective, the struggle is deemed more serious. Those who for whatever reason are suggesting that radical alternatives are possible have failed to listen to reason, can no longer be dismissed as misguided or deluded, and are now considered to be potentially if not actually dangerous. At this point, the rhetoricians of reaction reach for the final item in their toolkit: 'the jeopardy thesis'. Given that this is the last rhetorical ploy available, its use is carefully graduated from insinuation, through more or less veiled threat, to explicit threat. In its gentlest form, 'the jeopardy thesis' states that: 'the proposed change, though perhaps desirable in itself, involves unacceptable costs or consequences of one sort or another' (Hirschman 1991: 81). In its less gentle form, it suggests or claims that the proposed change may risk the security of the state or defy the supposed 'will of the people'. In its more extreme forms, it involves the prolonged public vilification and denunciation of the proponents of change through every outlet available. That is, increasingly, how Western democracy – as long as it remains within the bounds of supposedly reasonable argument rather than straying into violent suppression – defends itself against any attempt at genuine democratisation.

The genuinely democratic task remains what it always was and what Luxemburg insisted that it should be and would be: to expose and challenge the economic, civic and social bases of the existing order, and, in doing so, show that what is deemed to be the natural order of things is nothing of the kind. It was – and continues to be – made by human beings who had the power to shape human history according to their own vested interests. Having been made it can be unmade and remade, but only through the collective action and critical consciousness of those at the sharp edge of history: those who endure the suffering – both *la grande misère* and *la petite misère* – of economic, civic and social marginalisation. The prime task in the struggle for democratic renewal is to think differently and in so doing to think freedom – what it means, what it costs, what it is for – within and for the current context.

Thinking economic freedom

The evidence that austerity measures undertaken within a framework of neoliberal economic policies generate inequality is overwhelming (see, for example, Atkinson 2015, 2016; Piketty 2014, 2016; Stiglitz 2012, 2015). Similarly, the argument that such measures are not only unjust but at best ineffective and at worst counter-productive is irrefutable (see, for example, Blyth 2015; Krugman 2012, 2015; Liu 2015). The evidence is there. The arguments are incontrovertible. Neoliberalism and its outworn economic policies stagger on, but are increasingly besieged by reality. They are threadbare – as is, sadly, much of the social fabric that they leave behind as an enduring legacy of their ideological malignity.

But to understand the full impact of those policies, we need to dig down to the conception of economics that underpins them: the notion of a 'disembedded' economy that is self-sustaining and self-adjusting and that can be managed through the application of technical expertise and – in the UK, at least – the knowledge gained from a three-year combined degree at an Oxford College. (The much vaunted University of Oxford combined degree in philosophy, politics and economics has been a main route through to political preferment for the political elite in the UK and elsewhere.) It is an economy that by floating free from the mechanisms of public accountability is largely inscrutable. It also – and to an incalculable extent – relies on escalating levels of private debt particularly among the young and most vulnerable.

This general line of argument was advanced consistently and powerfully by the Hungarian political economist Karl Polanyi, whose life's vocation – as his biographer Gareth Dale (2016: 28) writes – 'was to subject the commercial ethic to moral critique and the market economy to scientific critique.' His magnum opus, *The Great Transformation*, provided both a history of market society and an analysis of how – by reducing citizens to egotistical incentive-seekers – such a society becomes increasingly atomised (see Polanyi 1944). With the market economy, he argued, came a new type of society and, crucially, a new conception of the economic:

> an 'economic sphere' came into existence that was sharply delimited from other institutions in society. Since no human aggregation can survive without functioning productive apparatus, this had the effect of making the 'rest' of society a mere appendage to that sphere. This autonomous sphere, again, was regulated by a mechanism that controlled its functioning. As a result, that controlling mechanism became determinative of the life of the whole body social ... 'Economic motives' now reigned supreme in a world of their own.
>
> (Polanyi 2014: 35)

Polanyi challenges the idea that markets and governments are separate and autonomous entities. An ungoverned market, Polanyi argues, is a market cut loose from its political and social moorings. While acknowledging that markets are necessary for any functioning economy, he insists that any attempt to create a 'market society' – a society based entirely on market principles and dependent on material goods alone – threatens the relational fabric of human life. It denies the very non-material goods – mutuality, reciprocity, recognition – that open up the possibility of a just society and a vibrant polity.

To view the economy as morally and politically 'disembedded' means seeing it as ethically disconnected in terms of self-realization and the fulfilment of individual potential.

The idea that the economy is an isolated and impermeable sphere was undoubtedly one of the factors contributing to the financial crisis of 2007/2008, which had much less to do with public expenditure and public deficits than with the way in which global banks were allowed to extend vast amounts of credit on the basis of very little core capital. Within the global economy, debt-fuelled speculation took precedence – and in many cases, continues to take precedence – over productive lending, with most of the money in the system being used for lending against existing assets. The banks took immense risks, were bailed out by the public when the risks failed to pay off, and paid huge bonuses to those responsible for the ensuing crisis, thereby squandering the trust and good will of the public. 'In an incredibly short space of time,' as James Meek comments, 'the banks swelled to grotesque size, then popped' (2016: 7).

At the same time, inequality escalated. 'Inequality,' in Sennett's view, 'has become the Achilles' heel of the modern economy' – the defining characteristic of 'the culture of the new capitalism' (2006: 54). The victory of freedom (as embodied in the free market) carried with it immense costs. David Harvey, in his depiction of the 1990s as a decade of 'corporate corruption' and 'scams and fraudulent schemes', spells out the cost to society exacted by the 'new capitalism': 'society seemed to be fragmenting and flying apart at an alarming rate. It seemed ... in the process of collapsing back into the aimless, senseless chaos of private interests' (Harvey 2003: 16–17). The extreme inequalities that characterise 'the new capitalism' impoverish everyone through their relentless erosion of the democratic space of civil society.

Economies that bestow such gains on small groups at the top are inherently unstable. They generate dissatisfaction and social unrest among those at the bottom that can – as is increasingly apparent across Europe and elsewhere – all too easily be channelled into forms of authoritarian populism and directed against vulnerable minorities including immigrants and those dependent on social welfare. In this way, the social consequences flowing from the 'disembedded' economy impact on the quality – and, ultimately, the very survival – of democratic politics. It is the unquestioned assumptions underlying the 'disembedded' economy, and the deleterious consequences that flow from it, that constitute the jeopardy – not those who challenge it and seek alternatives to it.

To *think* economic freedom is to think against and beyond the abstracted system of economic transactions – restricted and predetermined – that currently constitutes the 'disembedded' economy. It is to think both globally (e.g. transferring resources from richer to poorer countries in ways which did not entangle the latter in further conditional indebtedness) and locally (e.g. shifting towards wage-led and domestic demand-led growth through increased public expenditure and forms of social ownership within banking). It is to demand that governments make investments that transform their societies so as to create capacity, knowledge and long-term growth (see Ghosh, 2013, 2017; Mazzucato 2015, 2018). To begin to think against the grain of received economic opinion – to think differently – is a first crucial step towards imagining a world in which choice and autonomy are no longer the privilege of the few but are the birthright of all.

Thinking civic freedom

As citizens, we exercise choice and autonomy within what is often described as 'the public sphere' or 'public domain', within which we are 'publicly' accountable to one another as members of 'the public'. The problem with these phrases is that they suggest timeless and impermeable categories, when how, and to what extent, we exercise choice and autonomy as members of 'the public' depends on how 'the public' is being defined and by whom it is being prescribed. The idea of 'the public' is itself shaped by history and epoch: for example, within an unrestrained monarchy, 'the public' is little more than a body of office holders dependent on the Crown for status and courtly prestige; within a republic, on the other hand, 'the public' is an expanded 'body politic' of republican citizens endowed with political will and purpose; and within a modern late-capitalist democratic state 'the public' is literate and 'reasonable', critical in the defence and promotion of its own vested interests, and external to the direct exercise of political power.

The latter comprises a more or less informed electorate, for whom property, private ownership and the assumption of merit become the prime *raison d'être*. This modern construction of 'the public' is, as Dan Hind sees it, a 'public of private interests' that has produced what he calls 'the paradox of modern power, the fact of a secret public' (2010: 44). What holds this public together is its shared commitment to private gain: the public interest becomes an aggregate of private interests. This is a privatised – and a privatising – public, for whom, as Judt puts it, 'what is private, what is paid for, is somehow better for just that reason.' Judt points out,

> This is an inversion of a common assumption in the first two thirds of the [twentieth] century, certainly the middle fifty years from the 1930s to the 1980s: that certain goods could only be properly provided on a collective or public basis and were all the better for it.
>
> (Judt with Snyder 2012: 362)

The 'public of private interests' judges all questions of dispensability and indispensability according to the criterion of private interest. Its default position has been neatly satirised by Will Hutton: 'my property is my own because I and I alone have sweated my brow to get it; I have autonomy over it and no claim to share it, especially by the state, is legitimate' (2010: 183). Implicit in this default position is a particular notion of freedom, namely, freedom from all constraints that serve in any way to limit individual gain regardless of wider public interests. The state exists to protect that freedom, not to pursue policies that ensure the welfare of society as a whole. The idea of 'active' or 'big' government – or a state committed to 'social investment' – is deemed therefore to be incompatible with a 'public of private interests': a public whose atomised members remain quietly but determinedly protective of – though apparently blind to – the inequalities that support and perpetuate their own vested interests.

The supposedly classless society on which the idea of the 'public of private interests' is premised is in fact riddled with inequality: 'at the top', suggests Erik Olin Wright, is 'an extremely rich capitalist class and corporate managerial class, living at extraordinarily high consumption standards, with relatively weak constraints on their exercise of economic power'; at the bottom is 'a pattern of interaction between race and class in which the working poor and the marginalised population are disproportionately made up of racial minorities' (2009: 114). Power has become increasingly concentrated in a small and largely unaccountable elite, a new 'ruling class' for which – argues Harvey – the political class now acts as proxy: 'state and capital are more tightly intertwined than ever, both institutionally and personally. The ruling class, rather than the political class that acts as its surrogate, is now actually seen to rule' (2011: 219).

The 'public of private interests' is thus a public without a vibrant polity, a polity without a vibrant citizenry: a public the economic sustainability of which is based not only on pre-existing levels of inequality, but on escalating inequality. Caught in this web of contradictions, the citizen becomes perfectly adapted to what Wolin (2010) has termed 'the managed democracy': a democracy outsourced to an oligarchy comprising the super-rich, the political elite and corporate business. This 'managed democracy' relies not only on an acquiescent citizenry but also on institutions that are 'thin' in terms of engagement and participation and increasingly centralised with regard to both their internal management and audit structures and their external control and accountability systems. The civic spaces between the individual and the state – the institutional spaces of civic association that straddle the public and private – are thereby hollowed out by a combination of disengagement and bureaucratic managerialism and squeezed out by increased centralised control coupled with creeping privatisation (see Elliott and Atkinson 2016; Meek 2014).

To *think* civic freedom is to refuse to be an assenting member of a 'public of private interests', which prioritises private profit over public good. It is to demand that the government acts on behalf of the people, not one privileged section of it. It is to insist on measures that counter inequality and empower the most disadvantaged in society: measures that tackle gross inequalities in, for example, education, employment, health and housing and that provide a welfare system fit for purpose. But is also to acknowledge that democracy needs to be reconceived as something other than a form of government: as a mode of being that, as Wolin puts it, 'is a recurrent possibility as long as the memory of the political survives' (2016: 111). To think civic freedom is to hold open that possibility, and – in doing so – to imagine new ways of being together.

Thinking social freedom

As the public has been privatised, the social has become marketised. The ideology of individualism and competition that pervades the global market has seeped into the culture of almost all the major public institutions. Thirty-five years ago – in the early years of the Thatcher administration – Williams highlighted the extent of both the exploitation of the earth's natural resources and the spoiling of its social resources when he remarked on 'this orientation to the world as raw material [that] necessarily includes an attitude to people as raw material' (1983: 261). In the intervening years, that attitude has been fostered by unfettered consumerism, one obvious manifestation of which has been the profitable institutionalisation and normalisation of the pornographic depiction of the human body as 'raw material' (*The Sun* newspaper launched its first nude 'Page 3' spread on 17 November 1970).

The combination of individualism, competition and consumerism has generated mistrust, weakened social bonds and had a profound effect on the way we perceive ourselves and others. We have, for example, become particularly inventive in the cruelties we inflict upon ourselves: addiction to ever-new combinations of damaging drugs, eating disorders leading to obesity or life-threatening loss of weight, self-harming and self-disfigurement, and the like. Whatever the complex causes of these phenomena, they are a clear manifestation of something having gone badly wrong in the individual's relationship with her or his self. Quite simply, a lot of people for whatever reason seem not only to dislike themselves but to want to severely punish themselves. We have achieved, as Williams puts it, 'the improbable combination of affluent consumption and widespread emotional distress' (1983: 267).

It is, of course, not particularly helpful to ascribe our social disorders to generalities such as 'individualism', 'competition' and 'consumerism'. The causes of these disorders are multiple, complex and highly contested. However, what is incontestable is the *fact* of those disorders and the human suffering they entail. In the postscript to his and his team's magisterial study of the new forms of social suffering in contemporary France, Bourdieu argues that this suffering goes largely unrecognised because of the disjuncture between the social and the political:

> With only the old-fashioned category of 'social' at their disposal to think about these unexpressed and often inexpressible malaises, political organizations cannot perceive them and, still less, take them on. They could do so only by expanding the narrow vision of 'politics' they have inherited from the past and by encompassing ... all the diffuse expectations and hopes which, because they often touch on the ideas that people have about their own identity and self-respect, seem to be a private affair and therefore legitimately excluded from political debate.
>
> (Bourdieu *et al.* 1999: 627)

One of the interviewees who took part in the study was Lydia D. She was 35 and had worked for an industrial cleaning service as a cleaner (one of the sectors where the right to work is least assured). Following a restructuring of the industry she was laid off, as a result of which she and her husband lost their recently acquired home. She had gone through numerous training programmes, but had been unable to find work. At the time of the interview, she is living with her husband's family, who were deeply unsympathetic to both her and her husband, who after having been unemployed had been given insecure work in a nearby factory where he has to alternate between a 4am to 1pm shift and a 1pm to 9pm shift. 'Locked in the vicious circle of poverty,' writes Bourdieu,

> she cannot afford either the motorbike or the car that would allow her to take up job offers at the end of the training period (anyway she has neither a driver's license nor any way to prepare for the driving test).
>
> (Bourdieu *et al.* 1999: 371)

For Lydia D, the sharp edge of suffering is the sheer carelessness of the world: the constant deferment of benefit payments, the anonymous officials who pass her from one office to another and require her to fill out endless forms, her husband's family who refuse to sympathise with her and her husband's plight. The 'meanness' of the world makes no sense to her:

> I mean is this a life? There are times when I just want to give up, sometimes even, sometimes even, … I'm so tired of it all that I just want to dump everything right on the spot … And there are times when you wonder how come the world is made like this, because it used to be, the world didn't use to be so mean and even, when sometimes you go someplace just to ask for information, people send you packing, things like that, sometimes.
>
> (Lydia D, quoted in Bourdieu *et al.* 1999: 377)

Bereft of almost all the relationships that ensure social belongingness and cohesion, she is – as Bourdieu puts it – 'suspended between life and social death' (Bourdieu *et al.* 1999: 372).

To *think* social freedom is to think Lydia D. It is to acknowledge the reality of social suffering. It is to understand social exclusion and social marginalisation from the perspective of the excluded and marginalised, how they impact on individual lives and communities in particular circumstances, and how those circumstances differ across localities and regions. It is to be attentive to the specificity of social suffering. It is also to challenge those policies and initiatives that purport to address so-called 'social problems', but in fact only seek to contain or manage them. It is to contest any attempt to blame the suffering on the sufferers. To think social freedom is to draw the social into the orbit of the political.

THINKING AND ACTION

For Luxemburg, to think is to think *differently* and to act is to act *collectively*. To think what received opinion suggests we should think is to remain thoughtless; to act entirely on one's own is to remain powerless. When our capacity to think differently is combined with our capacity to act collectively, we discover our revolutionary potential. Luxemburg never prescribed an organisational framework for how that potential should be realized or a time-frame within which it should be actualised. She had no tactical ground plan tucked away in her back pocket for when the revolutionary moment arrived. In the articles and speeches she delivered in the final two months of her life, she specified the revolutionaries' demands and sketched out what she saw as some of the characteristics of a post-revolutionary democratic socialist society.

But nowhere does she seek to manage the process whereby those demands would be met or the conditions of democratic socialism be achieved. And nowhere does she associate the revolution with bloodshed and mob violence. On the contrary, she declares in one of her last articles published in *Die Rote Fahne*: 'The proletarian revolution requires no terror for its aims; it hates and despises killing' (R: 352).

For her, it was the relation between thinking and action that was crucial. Her recurring theme was: *think for yourselves and act together!* As she developed and elaborated that theme, she highlighted what she saw as some of the essential elements of the long revolution. They recur throughout her work.

We can see them as precepts which she herself seems to have lived by and which have continuing relevance.

The revolution belongs to everyone. It is yours and ours

Revolutionary struggles belong first or foremost to those who enact them. No person or group can assume ownership of the collective action that propels such struggles without reducing the revolutionary potential of that action. But revolutionary struggles belong not only to those who enact them, but to all those who in different places and at different times are inspired by them and for whom they symbolise the human capacity for resistance and hope. Thus, the spectators are drawn into the collective action. Together – in their own place and their own time – they sustain and carry forward the long revolution.

Take it a step at a time. Don't ever be defeated

The long revolution proceeds step by step. But the steps are not already in position as they would be if, say, we were climbing a ladder or making our way up a set of stairs. Each step is a step into the unknown. So in moving forward one has to think about the steps already taken. What may seem like a very small step at the time can – over time – open up huge possibilities. Those who fail – or refuse – to acknowledge those possibilities will judge your efforts futile. Some of them will write books about '*failed* revolutions' and '*lost* revolutions'. These books will become part of official history: a history you will reject.

Each step forward must broaden out and draw in

Collective action requires some measure of consensus regarding ends and means. Without it, the action dissipates and loses its collective power. But, unless the consensus accommodates the full diversity of the collective, it lacks legitimacy. So, as the collective expands and develops, it must constantly re-think and re-argue the consensus upon which it is based. If it fails to expand and develop – and to constantly re-think and re-argue – it will close in on itself and stultify. The process of broadening the constituency of struggle – and drawing in diverse voices and presences – constitutes the forward movement of revolutionary action.

Collective action shapes organisation

Organisation crystallises around collective action. Otherwise – as Luxemburg was swift to point out – organisation can get in the way. Deliberation, practical reasoning, thinking together: these are the key elements in this process of crystallisation. Organisation matters hugely. But collective action cannot be organised from the outside. To be sustainable it must be 'organic' in the sense of being organised from within and being responsive to changing circumstances. Rather than thinking of organisation and action as separate entities, we might think of collective action as a developing *organism*. Viewed in that way, the long revolution is not so much a matter of linear progression as of multi-dimensional growth.

Critical consciousness is holistic

Critical consciousness involves an understanding of the interconnectivity of things: then and now, here and there, us and them, I and you. It is through this process of making connections that critical consciousness moves from critique to enactment. The uniqueness of our own situation is located – and understood – within a broader context of solidarity and resistance. The internationalism that Luxemburg embraced was an expression of that solidarity and resistance and an acknowledgement that the shared reality of global exploitation impacts differentially across localities and regions. It is through our consciousness of shared suffering and sympathy that we move forward together.

The prime task is to gain confidence in our own energies and capacities. Only then are we able to challenge the supposed inevitabilities, and, by challenging them, begin to imagine the kind of world Luxemburg lived and died for: a world in which people – confident of their own capacities and energies – are able to face whatever new challenges lie ahead. Not an achieved utopia, but a world free of oligarchs and demagogues. A good world in the making.

Coda: 'I Was, I Am, I Shall Be'

In his novella, *The Three Lives of Lucie Chabrol*, John Berger (1992: 93–178) tells the story of Lucie, the daughter of peasant farmers and born in September 1900 in a village in the French Alps close to the Swiss border. She is unusually small in stature, but fearless and with piercing eyes the colour of forget-me-nots. Her nickname is 'Cocadrille', a legendary creature born supposedly from a cock's egg hatched in a dung heap. After the death of her parents, she continues to farm the smallholding with her two brothers. Her first life ends when the barn burns down one autumn morning and her brothers accuse her of deliberately setting fire to it.

During her second life, she lives in a derelict house on the outskirts of the village estranged from family and community. Throughout the spring and summer months, she collects food from the foothills and forests. In the hard winters, she knits for as long as there is enough light to do so. She smuggles what she can across the nearby border to sell in local markets where the exchange rate works in her favour. Her second life ends when she is murdered supposedly by an intruder, hoping to steal the small savings she has amassed over the years. She is 67 at the time.

At her funeral, the narrator – who is called Jean – hears her speaking to him in a whisper. Thus, begins the third life of Lucie Chabrol. Jean thinks the Cocadrille may have returned to name her murderer. But she tells him she is not interested in her killer. She has come – as the narrative reveals – not as a ghost to haunt, but as a questioning presence, a witness to past events, a possible guide to probable ways forward. She introduces Jean to some of those who, like her, met violent deaths. Saint-Just – a member of the French resistance murdered by the Nazis in a nearby village – tells Jean that 'Justice will be done'. 'When?' asks Jean. 'When the living know what the dead suffered,' replies Saint-Just.

So what of the three lives of Rosa Luxemburg? There was the long apprenticeship that ended, arguably, with the outbreak of the First

World War and her prolonged 'protective custody'; her entry into history on the streets of Berlin and her subsequent murder; and the afterlife of her words and deeds that continue to resonate 100 years after her death. She never wavered in her belief that justice would be done or in her commitment to exposing the suffering of those who were the victims of injustice and those who struggled against it. She carries no tablets of stone. We recall her as guide and witness – a questioning presence – not as a prophet.

She reminds us that the struggle against global injustice achieves realization not in some distant utopia but in the here and now. She reminds us also that revolutionaries are defined not by their membership of party, movement or creed, but by their determination to think critically and act collectively. They stand under no single banner and wear no single badge. Finally, she reminds us that the revolutionary struggle is not only 'out there' but also 'in here'. It exists as the potential for critical consciousness and collective action that exists within every human being: the revolution as the universal first person singular. '*I was, I am, I shall be*'.

Had Luxemburg lived to see the collapse of Europe into the totalitarian horrors of Nazism, she would, I think, have insisted on the enduring importance of certain liberal tenets: not least the idea that:

> Freedom only for the supporters of the government, only for the members of one party – however numerous they may be – is no freedom at all. Freedom is always and exclusively freedom for the one who thinks differently. Not because of any fanatical concept of 'justice' but because all that is instructive, wholesome and purifying in political freedom depends on this essential characteristic, and its effectiveness vanishes when 'freedom' becomes a special privilege.
>
> (R: 305)

And had she lived to see socialism collapse into the moral and political cesspit of Stalinism, she would – on the evidence of her fierce critique of Bolshevism – have insisted on the inextricable link between socialism and democracy: a democratic socialism grounded in both the ecological and humanistic thinking that radiates from her letters – particularly those written in prison to friends on the outside – and in her refusal to subordinate collective action to any kind of superimposed organisational framework.

She was far too intelligent to let truth slip on the grounds of ideological correctness. She brought everything – including bumblebees and flowers – into the rich mix of her political thinking. Standing at the threshold of 'the short twentieth century', she pointed a way forward towards a new kind of politics, a new way of being together, a new way of resisting the demagoguery and populism of our age. This was not because she was a utopian or a naive optimist. On the contrary, she was one of the few revolutionary leaders who had a genuinely tragic imagination, by which I mean she was able to confront the enormity of failure and catastrophe without recourse to any consolatory philosophy or false hope. For her – as for Williams – 'the revolution is an inevitable working through of a deep and tragic disorder' (1979b: 75).

Her strength lay in her capacity to see the past for what it was, to acknowledge its appalling consequences and to affirm that a better world is nevertheless possible.

As we confront what Judt in his final work warned would be 'a time of troubles' (2010: 207), it is worth recalling – and honouring – the intelligence and purity of Luxemburg's unfulfilled political vision of democratic socialism.

Glossary

The glossary is presented in three sections: key dates and events relating to Luxemburg's life and work; political organisations relating to those dates and events; and people referred to throughout the text.

DATES AND EVENTS

1871 **5 March**: Luxemburg born in Zamość in the province of Lublin, part of Russian-occupied Poland; youngest of five children; family speaks Polish and German at home with possibly some Yiddish.

1873 Family moves to Warsaw.

1875 German Social Democratic Party (SPD) established with the publication of the Gotha programme.

1876 Suffers hip condition; wrongly diagnosed as tuberculosis and, as a result, wrongly treated; confined to bed for a year; disabled for life.

1881 Tsar Alexander II assassinated following earlier assassination attempt in 1879.

1882 The *Proletariat* party, the first Polish Socialist party, founded by Ludwik Waryński.

1883 *Proletariat* organises strikes in Warsaw and Łódź and a general strike in Zyrardow; large-scale arrests follow and continue for the next two years.

1884 Enters girls' High School in Warsaw; all lessons and conversations in Russian; use of the Polish language strictly forbidden.

1886 Leading members of *Proletariat* imprisoned. Four of the leaders hanged in the Warsaw Citadel. Waryński sentenced to 16 years' hard labour – dies in custody three years later.

1887 Graduates from High School with As in 14 subjects and Bs in five. Denied traditional gold medal because of her supposedly rebellious attitude. Active in underground socialist groupings that constitute the remnants of *Proletariat*.

1889 **July:** Second International (1889–1916) formed in Paris; moves to Switzerland; registers at University of Zurich; meets Russian socialist exiles.

1890 Meets Leo Jogiches with whom she forms a long-term personal and political relationship.

1892 Founding of united *Polish Socialist Party* (PPS).

1893 **July:** first issue of *Sprawa Robotnicza* ('*The Workers Cause*') appears in Paris, with Jogiches providing funding for the paper.

August: addresses the Third Congress of the Second International in Zurich; distances herself from the PPS on the issue of Polish independence (which she opposes) and that of collaboration between the Polish and Russian working class (which she supports).

1893–1898: makes frequent visits to Paris to oversee the publication of *Sprawa Robotnicza* and to pursue her studies in the Polish libraries.

1894 Social Democracy and the Kingdom of Poland (SDKP) established by – among others – Luxemburg, Jogiches, Julian Marchlewski (pseudonym Karski) and Adolf Warszawski (Warski) as a breakaway from PPS. *Sprawa Robotnicza* becomes the policy organ of SDKP, with Luxemburg (using the pseudonym R. Kruszynska) taking over the editorship.

1896 **June:** final issue of *Sprawa Robotnicza* (No. 24) appears. Publishes articles highly critical of the PPS position on Polish nationalism in the chief theoretical organs of the German and Italian socialist parties.

July: leads the SDKP delegation at the Fourth Congress of the Second International in London; comes under fierce personal attack. SDKP's existence as a separate member of the International challenged but upheld.

1897 Awarded doctorate for thesis titled *The Industrial Development of Poland*.

Marries Gustav Lübeck in Basel, Switzerland, in order to gain permit for residency in Germany (They part immediately after the marriage ceremony and divorce five years later). Mother dies in Warsaw.

1898 **March**: First party congress of Russian Social-Democratic Labour Party (RSDLP).

May: moves to Berlin and joins SPD. Canvasses support for the SPD among the mostly Polish mine workers in Upper Silesia.

September: first of two series of articles published in *Leipziger Volkszeitung* ('*Leipzig People's Newspaper*') attacking Eduard Bernstein's revisionism.

September–November: edits *Sächsiche Arbeiterzeitung* ('*Saxon Workers' Newspaper*').

October: speaks twice at SPD congress in Stuttgart on the issue of 'revisionism'. Meets Clara Zetkin (1857–1933), lifelong friend and fellow activist.

1899 **April**: second of two series of articles published in *Leipziger Volkszeitung* attacking Bernstein's revisionism. The two series of articles are reprinted in book form as Part I of *Social Reform or Revolution*, along with a Part II that critiqued a highly influential work by Bernstein published earlier that year.

October: addresses SPD congress in Hanover; withdraws candidature for one of the editorial places at *Vorwärts* ('*Forward*'), the central organ of the SPD.

December: SDKP enlarged to form the Socialist Democracy of the Kingdom of Poland and Lithuania (SDKPiL).

1900 **April**: attends fifth Prussian PPS congress. Supports resolutions against Polish nationalism and for dissolution of PPS and absorption into the SPD.

August: Jogiches moves to Berlin, and, masquerading as her cousin, takes a room in the house where she lives.

September: argues against Polish nationalism at the SPD congress in Mainz. Attends Socialist International congress in Paris. Father dies in Warsaw. Summit conference between PPS and SPD. PPS refuse SPD demand to include either Luxemburg or Marcin Kasprzak (a party colleague with whom she had worked closely) on the editorial board of the Polish-controlled weekly paper, *Gazeta Robotnicza* ('*The Workers' Journal*').

1901   **April**: SPD executive proposes withdraw of financial support for *Gazeta Robotnicza*; September, SPD approves proposal at its annual congress in Lübeck.

October: Luxemburg invited to become joint editor (with Mehring) of *Leipziger Volkszeitung* following the death of its long-standing editor Bruno Schönlank.

1902   **April**: *Leipziger Volkszeitung* publishes 'A Tactical Question', her attack on the Belgian Social democrats for having agreed to drop their call for women's suffrage at the demand of the Liberals with whom they are in electoral coalition.

October: Luxemburg gives up all collaboration with the *Leipziger Volkszeitung* following a long-running quarrel with her co-editor and with the editorial board.

1903   Marriage to Lübeck dissolved. Becomes sole woman member of the International Socialist Bureau. Addresses Reichstag election rallies in Upper Silesia. Asked by editors of *Iskra* ('*Spark*'), a Menshavik-dominated journal, to analyse the split between the Mensheviks and the Bolsheviks in the Russian Social Democratic Party.

1904   Publishes 'Organisational Questions of Russian Social Democracy' in *Iskra* and *Neue Zeit* ('*New Times*') criticising Lenin's centralist party organisation.

July: sentenced to three months imprisonment for allegedly insulting the German Emperor and King of Prussia, William II, in her 1903 election campaign.

August: attends Socialist International Congress in Amsterdam as SPD and SDKPiL delegate. August: begins three-month prison sentence.

October: released from prison as part of the usual amnesty at the coronation of a new monarch, King Friedrich August of Saxony.

1905   Russian Revolution: wave of mass political and social unrest spreads through vast areas of the Russian Empire and Russian-partitioned Poland involving worker strikes, peasant unrest and military mutiny.

July: visits Jogiches for four weeks in Cracow where he has gone to organise SDKPiL activities.

September: calls on SPD at its congress in Jena to take up mass strike tactic. Returns to Cracow. Becomes an associate editor of *Vorwärts*.

December: moves to Warsaw as the revolution is subsiding.

1906 **March**: arrested in Warsaw with Jogiches.

July: released from custody on health grounds.

August: goes to Finland where she spends time with Lenin and his immediate Bolshevik circle.

Autumn: *The Mass Strike, the Political Party, and the Trade Unions* published as a pamphlet in Hamburg. Returns to Germany.

December, stands trial for remarks made at the SPD congress in Jena. Sentenced to two months imprisonment due to begin the following summer.

1907 **January**: Jogiches sentenced to eight years' hard labour in Siberia (following his arrest the previous year) – Luxemburg refuses to appear in person to answer the charges brought against her. Addresses rallies in Reichstag election campaign.

February: Jogiches escapes. Personal relations between Jogiches and Luxemburg end though they remain close political allies.

April: begins relationship with Konstantin Zetkin.

May: attends RSDLP congress in London as a delegate for both the SDKPiL and SPD – in a session chaired by Lenin, she evaluates the various tendencies in Russia in the light of the events of 1905. Meets Jogiches in person for first time since their arrest in Warsaw the previous year.

June–July: serves prison sentence as pronounced the previous December.

August: attends Socialist International Congress in Stuttgart and speaks in the name of the Polish and Russian delegations against militarism and imperialism. Addresses First International Conference of Socialist Women held simultaneously and in the same building.

October: becomes only female lecturer at the newly established SPD Central Party School in Berlin (courses run from the beginning of October to the end of March each year until the outbreak of the First World War).

1908 Begins work on *Introduction to Political Economy*, an unfinished book based on her lectures at the SPD Central Party School (incomplete text published posthumously in 1925).

September: defends the Central Party School at the SPD congress in Nürnberg.

1909 **May–July:** visits Italy spending time in Zurich on both the outward and return journeys.

August: ends relationship with Konstantin Zetkin. Correspondence between them maintained until a few months before her death.

1910 **February–March:** powerful upsurge of struggle by the German working class (including strikes, demonstrations and clashes with police) to end the Prussian three-class voting system and press for general suffrage.

March: submits an article titled 'What Next?' to *Vorwärts*, who refuse to publish it. Submits it to *Neue Zeit* where Karl Kautsky as editor refuses to publish a section on republicanism. Submits it to *Dortmunder Arbeiterzeitung* ('*Dortmund Workers' Newspaper*'), where it is finally published.

April–August: Kautsky takes issue with Luxemburg in an article ('What Now?') published in *Neue Zeit*, in which he argues that the time is not ripe for struggles outside the electoral, parliamentary arena. Luxemburg responds with 'Theory and Practice' in which she confronts Kautsky on issues relating to mass action and the relationship between spontaneity and organisation. Kautsky publishes her article in *Neue Zeit*. Public break with Kautsky.

September: attends SPD congress in Magdeburg where her mandate is challenged and she is isolated.

1911 **September–early October:** writes *Credo: On the State of Russian Social Democracy* (handwritten in Polish and never published during Luxemburg's lifetime).

1912 Works with great speed and intensity on *The Accumulation of Capital: A Contribution to the Economic Explanation of Capital*.

1913 *The Accumulation of Capital: A Contribution to the Economic Explanation of Capital* is published in German.

1914   **February**: sentenced to one year's imprisonment for incitement to disobedience but freed pending appeal – speech from dock published as *Militarism, War and the Working Class*.

     28 June: assassination of Archduke Franz Ferdinand in Sarejevo.

     28 July: declaration of war on Serbia by Austro-Hungary.

     31 July: declaration of war on Russia by Germany.

     2 August: invasion of Luxembourg by Germany.

     3 August: declaration of war on France by Germany and the invasion of Belgium by Germany.

     4 August: declaration of war on Germany by the UK and the decision by the parliamentary members of the SPD to vote for 'war credits'.

1915   **19 February**: begins serving sentence at the women's prison in Barnimstrasse in Berlin.

     February–April: writes *The Junius Pamphlet: The Crisis of Social Democracy* (first published as a pamphlet in Zurich, Switzerland).

1916   Completes *The Accumulation of Capital, Or, What the Epigones have Made of Marx's Theory – An Anti-Critique* (first published in 1921).

     August: released from prison. Rearrested and placed in custody again in Barnimstrasse and then in Wronke in German Poland. International Group (Spartacus Group) formed.

1917   **July**: transferred to Breslau Prison (now Wrocław) in west Poland.

1918   **September**: writes *The Russian Revolution* (unfinished on her release from prison and never published during her lifetime).

     5–12 November: 'Spartacus Week'.

     8 November: released from prison.

     10 November: travels from Breslau to Berlin.

     31 December: founding conference of KPD.

1919   **15 January**: Luxemburg murdered along with Liebknecht. Luxemburg's body thrown into the Landwehr canal.

     25 January: Liebknecht buried along with 32 others killed during 'Spartacus Week'

     10 March: Jogiches arrested and murdered

31 **May**: Luxemburg's body discovered washed up at one of the locks of the canal.

13 **June**: Luxemburg's funeral held at Friedrichsfelde Cemetery.

ORGANISATIONS

KPD Communist Party of Germany (Kommunistische Partie Deutschlands)

PPS Polish Socialist Party (Polska Partia Sozjalistyczna)

RSDRP Russian Social Democratic Workers' Party (Rossiyskaya Sotsial-Demokraticheskaya Rabochaya Partiya)

SDKP Social Democracy of the Kingdom of Poland (Socjaldemokracja Królestwa Polskiego)

SDKPil Social Democracy of the Kingdom of Poland and Lithuania (Socjaldemokracja Królestwa Polskiego i Litwy)

SEWA Self-Employed Women's Association (of India)

SPD Social Democratic Party of Germany (Sozialdemokratische Partie Deutschlands)

USPD Independent Social Democratic Party of Germany (Unabhängige Sozialdemokratische Partei Deutschlands)

PEOPLE

Bebel, Ferdinand August (1840–1913), leading member of the SPD; member of the Reichstag, 1867–1881 and 1883–1913; 1892–1913, co-chairman of the SPD; from 1889, a leading member of the Second International.

Bernstein, Eduard (1850–1932), political journalist; leading member of the SPD; lived in emigration in London, 1890–1901; member of the Reichstag, 1902–1906 and 1912–1918; resigned from the SPD on pacifist grounds over its support for the First World War; re-joined the SPD, 1919.

Diefenbach, Hans (1884–1917), physician; Luxemburg's lover for some years prior to 1915; killed in action during the First World War.

Ebert, Friedrich (1871–1925), became a member of the SPD Executive, 1905; member of the Reichstag, 1912–1918; a leading representative of reformism and a supporter of the First World War; became chairman of the Reichstag group of SPD deputies, 1916; named Chancellor of the German Empire, 9 November 1918; centrally involved in the crushing of the Spartacus League uprising ('Spartacus Week'), January 1919.

Friedrich II (1712–1786), King of Prussia, 1740–1786.

Frölich, Paul (1894–1953), left of SPD even before the First World War; opposed the First World War; leading member of the 'Left Radical' anti-First World War grouping; delegate to founding conference of the KPD, December 1919; expelled from KPD as 'rightist', 1928; arrested and freed after nine months, 1933; exiled in Czechoslovakia, Belgium, France and USA; author of biography of Luxemburg, 1939; returned to West Germany and joined SPD, 1950.

Jacob, Mathilde (1873–1943), acted as Luxemburg's secretary; became her friend and one of her main contacts with the outside world throughout Luxemburg's imprisonment during the First World War; author of a memoir of Luxemburg, first published in German in 1988 and translated into English in 2000.

Jogiches, Leo (1867–1919), Luxemburg's lover, early 1890s to 1907; co-founder of the SDKP (which in 1900 became the SDKPil), 1893; became co-editor of *Sprawa Robotnicza*, 1893; moved to Germany, 1900; co-founder and leading member of the International Group (Spartacus Group) and later the Spartacus League; member of the central committee of the KPD; arrested and murdered, March 1919.

Kautsky, Karl (1854–1938), co-founder and chief editor of the journal *Neue Zeit* until 1917; leading theoretician of the Second International; break with Luxemburg, 1910; co-founder of the USPD, 1917; returned to SPD in 1920; husband of Luise Kautsky.

Kautsky, Luise (1864–1944), Luxemburg's close and lifelong friend; wife of Karl Kautsky.

Levi, Paul (1883–1930), member of the International Group (Spartacus Group); Luxemburg's lawyer during the First World War; a leader of the KPD, 1918; expelled from the KPD, 1921;

published Luxemburg's *The Russian Revolution* after his expulsion from the party, 1922.

Liebknecht, Karl Paul August Friedrich (1871–1919), son of Wilhelm Liebknecht, a close friend and collaborator of Karl Marx; opened a law practice in Berlin in 1899 and specialised in defending fellow socialists in German courts; city councillor in Berlin, 1902–1913; member of the Prussian House of Deputies, 1908–1916; member of the Reichstag, 1912–1918; co-founder of the International Group (Spartacus Group) and later the Sparacus League; co-editor with Luxemburg of *Die Rote Fahne*; co-founder of the KPD; murdered, 15 January 1919.

Liebknecht, Sophie (1884–1964), art historian; second wife of Karl Liebknecht; close friend of Luxemburg.

Lübeck, Gustav (b. 1873), entered into a marriage of convenience with Luxemburg in order for her to gain Prussian/German citizenship, 1898; marriage officially dissolved, 1903; expelled from Switzerland as an 'anarchist', 1905.

Lübeck, Olympia (1851–1930), Polish-born friend of Luxemburg and mother of Gustav Lübeck.

Marchlewski, Julian Balthazar (1866–1925) co-founder of the Union of Polish Workers, 1889; helped produce the *Sprawa Robotnicza* together with Luxemburg, Jogiches and Warszawski, co-founder of the SDKP (which in 1900 became the SDKPiL), 1893; member of the staff of the *Leipziger Volkszeitung* and at times the editor, 1902–1913; co-founder of the International Group (Spartacus Group).

Mehring, Franz (1846–1919), literary scholar and historian; member of SPD; chief editor of *Leipziger Volkzeitung*, 1902–1907; colleague of Luxemburg in the SPD Party School in Berlin; co-founder of the International Group (Spartacus Group); co-founder of Spartacus League and the KPD.

Noske, Gustav (1868–1946), on the right wing of the SPD; minister of war, December 1918–March 1920; complicit in the murder of Luxemburg and likely to have delivered the order for her execution.

Pabst, Waldemar (1880–1970), member of the *Freikorps*; responsible for the murder of Liebknecht and Luxemburg; claimed to be acting on Noske's orders.

Roland Holst-van der Schalk, Henriette (1869–1952), Dutch writer and socialist; active in the women's movement; broke from both the Second International and the Dutch Social Democratic Party on the grounds of their reformism, 1909; became member of the Communist Party of Holland, 1918.

Scheidemann, Philip (1865–1939), SPD member of the Reichstag, 1903–1918; a leading advocate of reformism and during the First World War an arch militarist; co-chairman of the SPD with Ebert, 1917–1918; contributed significantly to the suppression of the revolution of 1918–1919 in Germany.

Vogel, Kurt (1889–1967) member of the *Freikorps*; involved in the murder of Liebknecht and Luxemburg.

Warszawski, Adolph (known as Warski) (1868–1937), co-founder of the Union of Polish Workers and the SDKPiL; worked on *Sprawa Robotnicza*, 1890–1896; representative of the SDKPiL in the central committee of the RSDRP, 1906–1912; co-founder of the Communist Workers' Party of Poland, 1918; married to Jadwiga Warski, Luxemburg's school friend.

Zetkin, Clara Josephine (1857–1933), close friend of Luxemburg; leading member of the SPD; chief editor of the Social Democratic women's' publication *Gleichheit*, 1892–1917; became secretary of the International Women's Secretariat, 1907; initiated the annual International Women's Day as a day of struggle for equal rights, peace and socialism, 1910; co-founder and leading member of the International Group (Spartacus Group) and later the Spartacus League. Leading member of the KPD from 1919 until her death.

Zetkin, Konstantin ('Kostya') (1885–1980), physician; son of Clara Zetkin; Luxemburg's friend and lover for several years after her break-up with Jogiches in 1907.

Notes

1. THE LONG APPRENTICESHIP

1. Hereafter referred to as *The Mass Strike*.
2. For the sake of consistency, I reference the version of *The Mass Strike* included in Hudis and Anderson (2004) – referenced as 'R' throughout. This version of Luxemburg's pamphlet includes Chapters 2, 3 and 4. The full text is included in Scott (2008: 111–181).

2. ENTERING HISTORY

1. Hereafter referred to as *An Anti-Critique*.
2. Hereafter referred to as *The Junius Pamphlet*.
3. See also Bessel 1993; Davis 2000; Diehl 1977; and Rosenhaft 1983.

References

Not all the works included in the references are cited in the text. This is particularly the case with regard to material relating to biographical details of and historical background to Luxemburg's life. The following brief note on the main sources used may therefore be helpful.

For the biographical details of Luxemburg's life, I have relied heavily on Nettl (1969), which remains a highly authoritative source in spite of the fact that new material has come to light since its publication (Ettinger 1986, draws on later material, but her account overall is less reliable than Nettl's). I have also drawn heavily on Frölich ([1939] 2010), who, although writing several years after Luxemburg's death, witnessed many of the events described. Jacob's (2000) account of her friendship with Luxemburg provides a further eyewitness account of events during the last five years of Luxemburg's life, while Salvadori (1990) offers some useful insights into the background to the dispute between Kautsky and Luxemburg. Cliff ([1959] 1983) is noteworthy if only because he offers a passionate and partisan defence of Bolshevism against the criticisms mounted by Luxemburg.

I also found Evans's (2015) graphic biography hugely compelling and helpful in establishing the narrative sweep of her life. Abraham (1989) and Bronner (1997) provide succinct introductions to her life and work. Harmer (2008) offers a brief – and not altogether sympathetic – biographical introduction, while Kaiser (2008) provides a stimulating but largely impressionistic account of some of the places that figured in Luxemburg's life. In bringing together a comprehensive selection of Luxemburg's letters, Adler, Hudis and Laschitza (2011) have provided a hugely important and highly accessible resource, which I have drawn on heavily throughout. Geras's ([1976] 2015) highly intelligent and scholarly discussion of the intellectual background to Luxemburg's thinking is indispensable.

For the historical background to her life, I drew on a range of sources, but found particularly useful: Craig (1981), Layton (2002) and Evans (2003) on the general background; Clark (2013) on the origins of the First World War; Gerwarth (2017) on events surrounding the end of the First World War and its aftermath; and Schorske (1955) on the history and development of German social democracy. Broué's ([1971] 2006), Carsten's (1972), Coper's (1955), Haffner's (1973), Harman's (1997), Ryder's (1967) and Ströbel's (1923) differing accounts of the German Revolution proved extremely useful, Haffner's was particularly so, since his own life and career as a leading journalist had been so entwined in the history of twentieth-century Germany.

The following abbreviations have been used in referring to the most frequently cited texts:

CW I – Hudis, P. (ed.) (2013) *The Complete Works of Rosa Luxemburg Volume I: Economic Writings 1*. Trans. D. Fernbach, J. Fracchia and G. Shriver. London: Verso.

CW II – Hudis, P. and Le Blanc, P. (eds) (2015) *The Complete Works of Rosa Luxemburg Volume II: Economic Writings 2*. Trans. N. Gray and G. Shriver. London: Verso.

L – Adler, G, Hudis, P. and Laschitza, A. (eds) (2011) *The Letters of Rosa Luxemburg*. Trans. George Shriver. London: Verso.

R – Hudis, P. and Anderson, K.B. (eds) (2004) *The Rosa Luxemburg Reader*. New York: Monthly Review Press.

RPL – Luxemburg, R. (2009) *Rosa Luxemburg: Selected Political and Literary Writings*. Revolutionary History 10(1). Pontypool, Wales: Socialist Platform Ltd. Merlin Press.

Abraham, R. (1989) *Rosa Luxemburg: A Life for the International*. Oxford: Berg.

Adler, G., Hudis, P. and Laschitza, A. (eds) (2011) *The Letters of Rosa Luxemburg*. Trans. George Shriver. London: Verso.

Adorno, T. ([1951] 2005) *Minima Moralia: Reflections on a Damaged Life*. Trans. E.F.N. Jephcott. London: Verso.

Ahmad, J. (2011) *The Wandering Falcon*. London: Hamish Hamilton by Penguin Books.

Appiah, K.A. (2005) *The Ethics of Identity*. Princeton, NJ: Princeton University Press.

Arendt, H. ([1958] 1998) *The Human Condition*, 2nd edn. Chicago, IL: University of Chicago Press.

Arendt, H. ([1963] 2006) *On Revolution*. London: Penguin.

Arendt, H. (1970) *Men in Dark Times*. London: Jonathan Cape.

Aronowitz, S. and DeFazio, W. (2010) *The Jobless Future*. 2nd edn. Minneapolis, MN: University of Minnesota Press.

Atkinson, A.B. (2015) *Inequality: What Can Be Done?* Cambridge, MA: Harvard University Press.

Atkinson, A.B. (2016) How to Spread Wealth: Practical Policies for Reducing Inequality. *Foreign Affairs* 95(1) (January/February): 29–33.

Badiou, A. with Tarby, F. (2013) *Philosophy and Event*. Trans. L. Burchill. Cambridge: Polity Press.

Bassiouni, M.C. (2016) Egypt's Unfinished Revolution, in A. Roberts, M.J Willis, R. McCarthy and T. Garton Ash (eds), *Civil Resitance in the Arab Spring: Triumphs and Disasters*. Oxford: Oxford University Press, 53–87.

Benjamin, W. ([1968] 2007) *Illuminations*. Trans. H. Zohn. Ed. H. Arendt. New York: Schocken Books.

Berger, J. (1992) *Into Their Labours: Pig Earth, Once in Europa, Lilac and Flag. A Trilogy*. London: Granta Books in association with Penguin Books.

Berger, J. (2016) *Landscapes: John Berger on Art*. Ed. T. Overton. London: Verso.

Bernstein, E. (1961) *Evolutionary Socialism: A Criticism and Affirmation*. Trans. E.C. Harvey. New York: Schocken Books.

Bessel, R. (1993) *Germany after the First World War*. Oxford: Oxford University Press.

Bhatt, A. and Bhatt, S. (2016) Microfinancing with SEWA Bank: Bringing Women into the Mainstream Economy. *Amity Business Review* 17(1) (January–June): 42–61.

Bluestone, B. and Harrison, B. (1984) *Deindustrialization in America: Plant Closings, Community Abandonment and the Dismantling of Basic Industry*. New York: Basic Books.

Blyth, M. (2015) *Austerity: The History of a Dangerous Idea*. Oxford: Oxford University Press.

Bourdieu, P. and Accardo, A., Balazs, G., Beaud, S., Bonvin, F., Bourdieu, E., Bourgois, P. Broccolichi, S., Champagne, P., Christin, R., Faguer, J.-P., Garcia, S., Lenoir, R., Œuvrard, F., Pialoux, M., Pinto, L., Podalydès, Sayed, A., Soilié, C., Wacquant, L.J.D. (1999) *The Weight of the World: Social Suffering in Contemporary Society*. Trans. P.P. Ferguson, S. Emanuel, J. Johnson and S.T. Waryn. Cambridge: Polity Press.

Bronner, S.E. (1997) *Rosa Luxemburg: A Revolutionary for Our Times*. University Park, PA: Pennsylvania State University Press.

Broué, P. ([1971] 2006) *The German Revolution*, 1917–1923. Ed. I. Birchall and B. Pearce. Trans. J. Archer. Chicago, IL: Haymarket Books.

Brynjolfsson, E. and McAfee, A. (2014) *The Second Machine Age: Work, Progress and Prosperity in a Time of Brilliant Technologies*. New York: Norton.

Carsten, F.L. (1972) *Revolution in Central Europe 1918–1919*. London: Temple Smithy.

Clark, C. (2013) *The Sleepwalkers: How Europe Went to War in 1914*. London: Penguin Books.

Cliff, T. ([1959] 1983) *Rosa Luxemburg*. London: Bookmarks Publishing Cooperative.

Conrad, J. (2007) *Heart of Darkness*. Ed. R. Hampson. London: Penguin Classics.

Cooper, R. (1955) *The Failure of a Revolution: Germany in 1918–1919*. Cambridge: Cambridge University Press.

Cowie, J. (2012) *Stayin' Alive: The 1970s and the Last Days of the Working Class*. New York: New Press.

Craig, Gordon (1981) *Germany, 1866–1945*. Oxford: Oxford University Press.

Crouch, C. (2011) *The Strange Non-Death of Neoliberalism*. Cambridge: Polity Press.

Dale, G. (2016) *Karl Polanyi: A Life on the Left*. New York: Columbia University Press.

Darwish, M. (2007) *The Butterfly's Burden*. Trans. F. Joudah Tarset. Northumberland: Bloodaxe Books.

Davis, B.J. (2000) *Home Fires Burning. Food, Politics, and Everyday Life in World War I Berlin*. Chapel Hill, NC: University of North Carolina Press.

Diehl, J.M. (1977) *Paramilitary Politics in Weimar Germany*. Bloomington, IN: Indiana University Press.

Dunne, J. (1997) *Back to the Rough Ground: Practical Judgement and the Lure of Technique*. Notre Dame, IN: University of Notre Dame Press.

Eiland, H. and Jennings, M.W. (2014) *Walter Benjamin: A Critical Life*. Cambridge, MA: Belknap Press of Harvard University Press.

Eliot, T.S. (2015) *The Poems of T.S. Eliot, Volume I: Collected and Uncollected Poems*. Ed. C. Ricks and J. McCue. London: Faber and Faber.

Elliott, L. and Atkinson, D. (2016) *Europe Isn't Working*. New Haven, CT: Yale University Press.

Ettinger, E. (1986) *Rosa Luxemburg: A Life*. Boston, MA: Beacon Press.

Evans, K. (2015) *Red Rosa: A Graphic Biography of Rosa Luxemburg*. Ed. P. Buhle. London: Verso.

Evans, R.J. (2003) *The Coming of the Third Reich*. London: Penguin.

Fischer, E. ([1959] 2010) *The Necessity of Art*. Trans. A. Bostock. London: Verso.

Frölich, P. ([1939] 2010) *Rosa Luxemburg: Ideas in Action*. Trans. J. Hoornweg. Chicago, IL: Haymarket Books.

Gadamer, H-G. (2001) *Gadamer in Conversation: Reflections and Commentary*. Ed. and Trans. R.E. Palmer. New Haven, CT: Yale University Press.

Gadamer, H-G. (2004) *Truth and Method*, 2nd revised edn. Trans. J. Weinsheimer and D.G. Marshall. London: Continuum (1st edn Germany, 1960).

Geras, N. ([1976] 2015) *The Legacy of Rosa Luxemburg*. London: Verso.

Gerwarth, R. (2017) *The Vanquished: Why the First World War Failed to End, 1917–1923*. London: Penguin Books.

Ghosh, J. (2013) Act Now! The Manifesto: A New Agenda for Global Economic Policies, in Flassbeck, H., Galbraith, J.K., Ghosh, J. Davidson,

P. and Koo, R. (eds), *Economic Reform Now: A Global Manifesto to Rescue Our Sinking Economies*. New York: Palgrave Macmillan, 161–173.

Ghosh, J. (2017) There is an Alternative. *Red Pepper* 215 (August/September): 24–27.

Gortz, A. (1982) *Farewell to the Working Class*. Trans. M. Sonencher. London: Pluto Press.

Gramsci, A. (1971) *Selections from the Prison Notebooks of Antonio Gramsci*. Ed. and Trans. Q. Hoare and G.N. Smith. London: Lawrence and Wishart.

Haffner, S. (1973) *Failure of a Revolution: Germany 1918–1919*. Trans. G. Rapp. London: André Deutsch.

Hagemann, K. (2002) Home/Front: The Military, Violence and Gender Relations in the Age of the World Wars, in K. Hagemann and S. Schüler-Springorum (eds), *Home/Front: The Military, War and Gender in Twentieth-Century Germany*. Oxford: Berg, 1–41.

Hawkins, N. (2002) *The Starvation Blockades: Naval Blockades of World War 1*. Barnsley: Leo Cooper.

Harman, C. (1997) *The Lost Revolution: Germany 1918 to 1923*. Revised Edition. London: Bookmarks (1st edn 1982).

Harmer, H. (2008) *Rosa Luxemburg*. London: Haus Publishing.

Harvey, D. (2003) *The New Imperialism*. Oxford: Oxford University Press.

Harvey, D. (2011) *The Enigma of Capital and the Crises of Capitalism*. London: Profile Books.

Hind, D. (2010) *The Return of the Public*. London: Verso.

Hirschman, A.O. (1970) *Exit, Voice, and Loyalty: Responses to Decline in Firms, Organizations, and States*. Cambridge, MA: Harvard University Press.

Hirschman, A.O. (1991) *The Rhetoric of Reaction: Perversity, Futility, Jeopardy*. Cambridge, MA: Belknap Press of Harvard University Press.

Holborow, M. (2015) *Language and Neoliberalism*. London: Routledge.

Honneth, A. (2017) *The Idea of Socialism: Towards a Renewal*. Trans. J. Ganahl. Cambridge: Polity Press.

Hudis, P. (ed.) (2013) *The Complete Works of Rosa Luxemburg Volume I: Economic Writings 1*. Trans. D. Fernbach, J. Fracchia and G. Shriver. London: Verso.

Hudis, P. and Anderson, K.B. (eds) (2004) *The Rosa Luxemburg Reader*. New York: Monthly Review Press.

Hudis, P. and Le Blanc, P. (eds) (2015) *The Complete Works of Rosa Luxemburg Volume II: Economic Writings 2*. Trans. N. Gray and G. Shriver. London: Verso.

Hutton, W. (2010) The Financial Crisis and the Need of the Hunter Gatherer, in R. Williams and L. Elliott (eds), *Crisis and Recovery: Ethics, Economics and Justice*. Houndmills: Palgrave Macmillan, 182–189.

Hyvönen, A-E. (2014) From Event to Process: The EU and the 'Arab Spring', in D. della Porta and A. Mattoni (eds), *Spreading Protest: Social Movements in Times of Crisis*. Colchester: ECPR Press, 91–116.

Iskandar, A. (2013) *Egypt in Flux: Essays on an Unfinished Revolution*. Cairo: The American University in Cairo Press.

Jacob, M. (2000) *Rosa Luxemburg: An Intimate Portrait*. Trans. H. Fernbach. London: Lawrence and Wishart in association with Heretic Books (1st edn Germany, 1988).

Judt, T. (2010) *The Memory Chalet*. London: William Heinemann.

Judt, T. with Snyder, T. (2012) *Thinking the Twentieth Century*. London: Heinemann.

Kaiser, I. (2008) *Rosa and the Wolves: Biographical Investigation into the Case of Rosa Luxemburg*. Trans. P.H. Stanley. Bloomington, IN: iUniverse.

Keynes, J.M. ([1919] 2007) *The Economic Consequences of the Peace*. New York: Skyhorse Publishing (1st edn London: Macmillan, 1919).

Krugman, P. (2012) *End This Depression Now*. New York: Norton.

Krugman, P. (2015) The Austerity Delusion. *The Guardian*, 29 April, 31–33.

Layton, G. (2002) *From Bismarck to Hitler: Germany 1890–1933*. London: Hodder and Stoughton.

Liebknecht, K. ([1907] 2012) *Militarism and Anti-Militarism*. Montreal: Black Rose Books.

Liu, L.L. (2015) *The Austerity Trap: Economic and Social Consequences of Fiscal Consolidation in Europe*. CreateSpace Independent Publishing Platform.

Lukács, G. ([1968] 1971) *History and Class Consciousness: Studies in Marxist Dialectics*. Trans. R. Livingstone. London: Merlin Press.

Luxemburg, R. (2009) *Rosa Luxemburg: Selected Political and Literary Writings*. Revolutionary History 10(1). Pontypool, Wales: Socialist Platform Ltd. Merlin Press.

Mason, P. (2015) *Postcapitalism: A Guide to the Future*. London: Penguin.

Mazzucato, M. (2015) *The Entrepreneurial State: Debunking Public vs. Private Sector Myths*, revised edn. London: Anthem Press.

Mazzucato, M. (2018) *The Value of Everything: Makers and Takers in the Global Economy*. London: Penguin.

Meek, J. (2014) *Private Island: Why Britain Belongs to Someone Else*. London: Verso.

Meek, J. (2016) Robin Hood in a Time of Austerity. *London Review of Books* 38(4) (18 February): 3–8.

Müller, J-W. (2016) *What is Populism?* Philadelphia, PA: University of Pennsylvania Press.

Ness, I. (2016) *Southern Insurgency: The Coming of the Global Working Class.* London: Pluto Press.

Nettl, P. (1969) *Rosa Luxemburg*, abridged edn. London: Oxford University Press (First published as two volumes in 1966 and 1969 respectively).

Nussbaum, M.C. (2000) *Women and Human Development: The Capabilities Approach.* Cambridge: Cambridge University Press.

Nye, A. (1994) *Philosophia: The Thought of Rosa Luxemburg, Simone Weil, and Hannah Arendt.* New York: Routledge.

Osborne, E.W. (2004) *Britain's Economic Blockade of Germany, 1914–1919.* London: Frank Cass.

Phillips, H. and Killingray, D. (eds) (2003) *The Spanish Influenza Pandemic of 1918–1919: New Perspectives.* London: Routledge.

Piketty, T. (2014) *Capital in the Twenty-First Century.* Trans. A. Goldhammer. Cambridge, MA: Belknap Press of Harvard University Press.

Piketty, T. (2016) *Chronicles: On Our Troubled Times.* Trans. S. Ackerman. New York: Viking.

Polanyi, K. (1944) *The Great Transformation: The Political and Economic Origins of Our Time.* New York: Farrar and Rinehart.

Polanyi, K. (2014) *For a New West: Essays, 1919–1958.* Ed. G. Resta and M. Catanzariti. Cambridge: Polity Press.

Rancière, J. (2006) *Hatred of Democracy.* Trans. S. Corcoran. London: Verso.

Rancière, J. (2007) *On the Shores of Politics.* Trans. L. Heron. London: Verso.

Roberts, A. (2016) Civil Resistance and the Fate of the Arab Spring, in A. Roberts, M.J. Willis, R. McCarthy and T. Garton Ash (eds), *Civil Resistance in the Arab Spring: Triumphs and Disasters.* Oxford: Oxford University Press, 270–325.

Roberts, A., Willis, M.J., McCarthy, R. and Garton Ash, T. (eds) (2016) *Civil Resistance in the Arab Spring: Triumphs and Disasters.* Oxford: Oxford University Press.

Rose, J. (2011) What More Could We Want of Ourselves! *London Review of Books* 33(12) (June): 5–12.

Rose, K. (1993) *Where Women Are Leaders: The SEWA Movement in India.* London: Zed Books.

Rosenhaft, E. (1983) *Beating the Fascists? The German Communists and Political Violence, 1929–1933.* Cambridge: Cambridge University Press.

Ryder, A.J. (1967) *The German Revolution of 1918: A Study of German Socialism in War and Revolt.* Cambridge: Cambridge University Press.

Said, E.W. (1978) *Orientalism.* London: Routledge and Kegan Paul.

Said, E.W. (1993) *Culture and Imperialism.* London: Chatto and Windus.

Said, E.W. (2004) *Humanism and Democratic Criticism.* New York: Columbia University Press.

Salvadori, M. (1990) *Karl Kautsky and the Socialist Revolution 1880–1938*. Trans. Jon Rothschild. London: Verso (1st edn Milan, 1976).

Savage, M., Cunningham, N., Devine, F., Friedman, S., Laurison, D., McKennzie, L., Miles, A., Snee, H. and Wakeling, P. (2015) *Social Class in the 21st Century*. London: Penguin.

Schorske, C.E. (1955) *German Social Democracy 1905–1917: The Development of the Great Schism*. Cambridge, MA: Harvard University Press.

Scott, H. (ed.) (2008) *The Essential Rosa Luxemburg: Reform or Revolution and the Mass Strike*. Chicago, IL: Haymarket Books.

Scott, H. (2010) Rosa Luxemburg's *Reform or Revolution* in the Twenty-First Century. *Socialaist Studies, Études Socialistes* 6(2): 118–140.

Sennett, R. (1999) *The Corrosion of Character: The Personal Consequences of Work in the New Capitalism*. New York: W.W. Norton and Co.

Sennett, R. (2006) *The Culture of the New Capitalism*. New Haven, CT: Yale University Press.

Soueif, A. (2004) *Mezzaterra: Fragments from the Common Ground*. London: Bloomsbury.

Soueif, A. (2012) *Cairo My City: Our Revolution*. London: Bloomsbury.

Standing, G. (2011) *The Precariat: The New Dangerous Class*. London: Bloomsbury.

Stiglitz, J.E. (2012) *The Price of Inequality: How Today's Divided Society Endangers Our Future*. New York: Norton.

Stiglitz, J.E. (2015) *The Great Divide: Unequal Societies and What We Can Do About Them*. New York: Norton.

Stephenson, S. (2009) *The Final Battle: Soldiers of the Western Front and the German Revolution of 1918*. Cambridge: Cambridge University Press.

Streeck, W. (2016) *How Will Capitalism End? Essays on a Failing System*. London: Verso.

Streeck, W. (2017) *Buying Time: The Delayed Crisis of Democratic Capitalism*, 2nd edn. Trans. P. Camiller and D. Fernbach. London: Verso.

Ströbel, H. (1923) *The German Revolution and After*. Trans. H.J. Stenning. London: Jarrods Publishers.

Vincent, C.P. (1985) *The Politics of Hunger: The Allied Blockade of Germany, 1915–1919*. Athens, OH: Ohio University Press.

Williams, R. (1977) *Marxism and Literature*. Oxford: Oxford University Press.

Williams, R. (1979a) *Politics and Letters: Interviews with New Left Review*. London: New Left Books.

Williams, R. (1979b) *Modern Tragedy*. London: Verso.

Williams, R. (1980) *Problems in Materialism and Culture: Selected Essays*. London: Verso.

Williams, R. (1983) *Towards 2000*. London: Chatto and Windus/The Hogarth Press.

Williams, R. (1989) *Resources of Hope: Culture, Democracy, Socialism*. Ed. R. Gable. London: Verso.

Wolin, S.S. (2010) *Democracy Incorporated: Managed Democracy and the Specter of Inverted Totalitarianism*. Princeton, NJ: Princeton University Press.

Wolin, S.S. (2016) *Fugitive Democracy and Other Essays*. Ed. Nicholas Xenos. Princeton, NJ: Princeton University Press.

Wright, E.O. (2009) Understanding Class: Towards an Integrated Analytical Approach. *New Left Review* 60 (November/December): 101–116.

Žižek, S. (2014) *Event: A Philosophical Journey Through a Concept*. London: Penguin Random House.

Index

Printed and bound by CPI Group (UK) Ltd, Croydon, CR0 4YY

09/06/2025

14685871-0002